TOXIC FARTS

BRAIN-EATING AMOEBAS, MOSQUITO ASSASSINS
& MORE

297

Is

D1531387

MOTHER NATURE'S A BITCH...

A plant that melts your skin. Bacteria that devours your brain. Death by cat urine.

Despite what climate scientists might suggest, in the arms race to determine whether humanity or the rest of life on this planet will come out on top, **we are outgunned, outnumbered and outright doomed.** Sure, we have bug spray and Lysol and lawn mowers, but as a famous fake mathematician once opined, "Life, uh, finds a way." And in this case, plenty of the life on Earth seems specifically engineered to find a way to end yours. *This book is a collection of the most diabolical, debilitating and downright disgusting dealers of death on the planet and will absolutely help keep you alive— because you'll never want to leave your house.*

Just make sure you clean the litter box.

TABLE OF CONTENTS

KILLER CRITTERS

A golf ball–size octopus with a bite 1,000 times more lethal than cyanide; a big cat that'll stalk you on your walk home from the bar; a human-sized bird that'll use its 4-inch claws to shank you. Whether by sea, land or air, wherever you go, there's a creature waiting to end your life—especially if you're busy shoving an iPhone in its face. Don't get maimed for the 'Gram, and steer clear of these formidable foes.

Killer Critters

BLUE-RINGED OCTOPUS

Some people would think a **golf ball-sized, eight-armed creature covered in psychedelic blue rings is cute**—especially when you spot it calmly hanging out in a tide pool. Assuming that tiny + adorable = harmless, those same people might even pick up that colorful little octopus just to take pictures of how easily it fits in the palm of their hand. *As you've probably guessed by now, those people are idiots.*

All octopuses are venomous to a degree, but the **blue-ringed octopus is one of the most venomous creatures in the ocean.** *If it bites you, you're probably a goner*—not only is this octopus bite usually painless, meaning you might not realize what has happened until it's too late, **its venom is 1,000 times stronger than cyanide.** For those keeping score at home, just a little cyanide can kill you.

The octopus's venom, a neurotoxin called **tetrodotoxin,** quickly blocks nerve signals in the body, leading to **muscle numbness, nausea and vision loss, plus loss of senses and motor skills.** Eventually its victim will experience muscle paralysis, including the muscles needed to breathe. Luckily for humans, this isn't necessarily fatal as long as the victim receives artificial respiration immediately.

Currently, there is no known antidote for tetrodotoxin. But on the plus side, prevention is pretty easy—the blue-ringed octopus isn't particularly aggressive and has only been known to bite people if it's been cornered or feels threatened. *So as long as you don't poke, pick up or otherwise get too close to one, you should be safe.*

6 Toxic Farts, Brain-Eating Amoebas, Mosquito Assassins & More

In 2018, a girl playing on a beach in Western Australia took home some seashells. After she got home, her aunt decided to wash the shells and discovered a blue-ringed octopus hiding in one of them. Thankfully no one was hurt, but bites from these tiny terrors have killed at least three people in Australia, and nearly killed many others.

LIONFISH

With their zebra-like stripes and long fins that evoke the look of a lion's mane, these fish are mesmerizing to look at. But like many things in the wild, it's best to look and not touch—**lionfish have multiple defensive, venomous spines ready to knock you or any other predator out**.

Lionfish have three kinds of venomous spines: dorsal, pelvic and anal. (*Yes, anal.*) The sting itself isn't fatal to humans—some victims report pain and tingling sensations for days or weeks. But if the venom travels to other parts of the body, you may experience **chills, cramps, headaches and nausea**. Oh, and paralysis and seizures. *And since you likely got stung in the water, you might drown.*

SWELL ADVICE

If you've been stung in an area where you're wearing jewelry, take it off immediately. The area will swell, meaning doctors may have to cut that wedding ring off to save your finger.

PIRANHA

Despite the rumor you heard in middle school that a pack of piranhas can pick a human body clean in minutes, death by piranha is extremely rare. Still, that doesn't mean these **razor-toothed fish** aren't worth fearing.

Usually, piranhas seek out prey smaller than themselves. But they also don't discriminate between things like fingers, feet and other fish. Even the smaller species of piranha can cause quite a bit of pain: *one 6-inch-long variety is also known as "white bitche" in Brazil.*

When one member in a school of piranha finds some likely prey, it alerts the rest of the group, which then **takes turns swooping in and taking bites out of some poor creature or human limb**. And because they travel in shoals for self-preservation, those bites can add up.

CROCODILE

According to *National Geographic*, saltwater crocodiles can weigh up to 2,200 pounds and reach lengths of 23 feet. They also have the **strongest bite ever measured**—scientists think the jaw strength of these reptiles might rival that of the T. rex. Specifically, their jaws clamp down with a **"bite force"** of 3,700 pounds per square inch. By comparison, lions have a bite force of 1,000 psi, and humans bite into a steak with about 150 to 200 psi. In other words, if one of them gets its jaws around your leg, it's gonna leave a mark—*assuming it doesn't cleave the limb right off your body.*

Also, because crocs can't chew, they've instead developed the technique of something scientists have dubbed the **"death roll,"** meaning **they bite down and twist their entire bodies over and over in order to dismember and kill their prey**. Thankfully, this is something that rarely gets done to humans, but that's only because most of us stay as far as we can from crocodiles.

Of course, your chances of death or dismemberment increase quite a bit if you purposefully work with these death-dealers up close. On New Year's Eve 2016, one overzealous crocodile trainer in Thailand experienced the **infamous death roll** while a horrified audience watched. After sticking his hand into the croc's mouth for some reason he surely now regrets, the crocodile bit down and flipped over, tossing the trainer around and **completely mangling his arm**.

COWS (AND THEIR TOXIC FARTS)

As you can likely imagine, standing downwind from a gassy cow isn't a pleasant experience. And most cows are gassy—a cheap diet of corn and soy keeps their wind breaking and burps bubbling even more than if they were to eat a more natural diet of alfalfa and other local vegetation.

Unfortunately for us, cow farts (and belches) are more than just olfactorily offensive—**they're a significant producer of methane, a powerful greenhouse gas.** Cows, like other grazers, get some help from gut microbes to help break down the tough grasses they eat. These microbes then create methane in their own waste, which the cows burp or toot into the environment.

According to *National Geographic*, **methane is 28 times more effective than carbon dioxide at trapping heat and raising the Earth's temperature over the course of 100 years.** Of course, there are many natural and human-made sources of methane in the world (see Bogs on page 107 and Climate Change on page 226), but the global addiction to cheeseburgers and milkshakes isn't exactly helping—cows and other grazers are responsible for about **40 percent** of the world's annual methane allotment. **There are currently about 1.4 billion cattle in the world and that number is expected to rise** as people continue scarfing down beef burritos and attempting to complete 76-ounce steak challenges, which in turn exponentially increases the world's number of toxic cow *(and, let's be honest, human)* farts. That's bad news for the environment and anyone among us who enjoys breathing clean air.

COWS (FALLING THROUGH ROOFS)

Though cows' natural digestive systems spell *(and smell)* bad news for humanity in the long term, one Brazilian bovine took a more direct approach to culling the human race. In 2013, in what was perhaps some sort of retaliation for decades of cow-tipping practices, **a rogue Brazilian farm cow escaped from its enclosure and climbed onto the roof of a neighbor's house.** The roof proved unable to support the 3,000-pound animal, sending it crashing onto the bed of a man and his wife. Miraculously, the wife and cow were fine, but the man died as a result of internal bleeding caused by the impact.

If you weren't already convinced that livestock don't belong on roofs, let us reassure you: they don't. In 2014, a man in Turkey bought a goat to be sacrificed for Eid al-Adha and, without a better place to put the animal until the festival, left it on the roof of his six-floor apartment building. Though there was a fence on the roof, **the goat still managed to make a fatal leap. The situation was made doubly tragic when the man's 13-year-old son—who was playing outside the building—broke the goat's fall.**

BEARS

Like most incredibly dangerous animals, bears are likely to leave you alone as long as you extend them the same courtesy (*and don't tempt them to your campsite or home by leaving food out in the open*). Bears are also known to get pissy when surprised, however, so if you are hiking through bear country, be sure to wear a bell. If you do cross a bear—or worse, **get between a mother bear and her cubs**—things can get very, very ugly.

In 2018, a Pennsylvania woman was **attacked by a bear outside her home and dragged for 88 yards**. Authorities aren't sure why the attack happened, though they suspect the bear's cubs were nearby or it was attracted to deer body parts that were in the woman's yard. (*Tip: Store your leftover deer parts in sealed containers.*) Thankfully, the woman's **Chihuahua** attacked and distracted the bear, allowing her to get away.

Authorities suggest if you do see a bear, the best reaction is to move away slowly and sideways—do not run. And if the bear looks like it's about to attack you, do not play dead. Instead, wave your arms around, yell and generally make yourself look as big and threatening as possible so the bear decides you're not worth the risk. It really doesn't take a ton to make a bear give up a fight, as you might have guessed after reading about that heroic Chihuahua.

HIPPOPOTAMUS

If you're ever on an African safari, you probably think your biggest threat is becoming lion food or getting caught in a wildebeest stampede. But without a doubt, *you should be much more afraid of hippos*. According to BBC News, **these tusked terrors kill about 500 people per year in Africa**.

This statistic is so high for a few reasons. Though you might imagine they're happy-faced, marble-munching softies, *in real life hippos are aggro assholes known to attack anything in their way*, be it a crocodile or a boat full of people that got too close. Their territorial nature, combined with the fact that hippos have **surprisingly sharp teeth** and are the **third-largest land mammals on Earth**, weighing up to 6,000 pounds, makes them a threat to anything in their path. Still think they're just misunderstood? Picture this: Hippos also secrete an oily red substance that protects them from the blazing sun, but also makes them look like they're covered in blood. *In general, herbivores shouldn't look like they're smeared in gore.*

You might be thinking *"Well, I'll just stay out of the water,"* but that isn't really an option for those who use the rivers for fishing, bathing and laundry, such as the people who live in Gouloumbou, a village in Senegal. As village chief Abdoulaye Barro Watt told *The Washington Post*, **"They are evil monsters that attack us night and day**."

ELEPHANTS

Elephants are really, really big. Considering they can grow up to 13 feet tall and weigh up to 12,000 pounds, we probably should have figured there isn't really enough room on the planet for the both of us—*at least, not at the rate humans are going.*

According to *National Geographic*, elephant attacks have been on the rise in the 21st century. This is directly tied to the fact that as human populations increase and farmers are forced to expand their fields, elephant habitats are shrinking, forcing more conflicts (read: tramplings) between humans and elephants.

Interestingly, Caitlin O'Connell-Rodwell, a biologist at Stanford University, says **elephant territory battles rarely come to extreme violence**. As she explains it, normal elephant tiffs are "nothing like what is happening in India, with elephants killing farmers on a very frequent basis." Similarly, elephant researcher Joyce Poole has heard about elephants purposefully killing humans and has suggested these are "**elephants who have suffered some severe trauma at the hands of man.**"

Which leads us to the obvious question: *Are we living in a world where elephants are about to take revenge Hitchcock-style, à la The Birds*? One thing's for sure—elephants never forget.

TSETSE FLY

A bite from a tsetse fly is hard to miss. Unlike mosquitoes, which can draw blood without you noticing, **a tsetse fly's creepy little mouth is serrated,** *helping it saw its way under your skin to get to your blood.*

That's not even the worst part: tsetse flies also act as *tiny delivery systems for parasites* that cause **human African trypanosomiasis,** aka "sleeping sickness." Symptoms are typical of your average sickness: **fever, headaches, muscle aches** and—as the name suggests—a desire to nap. But as the parasite gets comfy and infection continues, you may also experience **personality changes, loss of coordination and extreme confusion.**

If victims aren't treated, **the infection is usually fatal.** However, there are also risks to treating sleeping sickness—some medications are toxic and can even be deadly, *especially if the parasite has already infected the victim's brain.*

RHINOCEROS

With a top speed of around **35 miles per hour** and **sharp horns on the fronts of their faces,** a charging rhino is a serious threat to your life—*and your car.* This is something tourists in drive-through safaris are reminded of every so often, when rhinos occasionally do their best to flip a car driving through their territory.

Of course, what's worse than having a rhino attack while you're in your car is having a rhino attack after you've gotten out of your car to take a picture. In 2013, **24-year-old Chantal Beyer was gored by a white rhino** while doing just that on a safari in South Africa. After the park owner apparently encouraged Beyer and her husband to *move closer to the deadly rhinos for a photo op,* one attacked and, according to the local *Beeld* newspaper, **"penetrated her chest from behind, causing a collapsed lung and broken ribs."** Miraculously, Beyer quickly received treatment and survived, which is great news. No one wants their last words to be *"Cheeeeeeeese—oh s*** a rhino!"*

LION

Weighing up to 420 pounds and armed with sharp claws and teeth, lions have always enjoyed being animals without any natural predators. Yet somehow, humans who have "tamed" (or at least, trapped) lions often seem to forget the very obvious fact that *these giant cats are much more powerful than we are.*

As usual, lions are much more likely to kill or maim people who can't keep their distance. And, as usual, some people learn this the hard way. One such man was 55-year-old Pieter Nortjé, who in 2019 stuck his arm through an electric fence to pet the wild creatures at the Tikwe River Lodge in Virginia, South Africa. After one lion didn't object to Nortjé petting him, the man waved over another, pushing his luck even further by calling, "Come here lovey, let daddy stroke you." *In a move anyone could have predicted*, the lion instead **bit his forearm, sinking its teeth down to the bone, attempting to drag him closer.** Luckily for Nortjé the lion let go after a few seconds and he survived after being treated for his injuries and septic shock.

TIGER

Tigers are streamlined killing machines that are known to enter Indian villages and snag a person for a quick meal. In fact, **tigers have killed at least 373,000 people in the last 200 years**, mostly in South and Southeast Asia.

Some 436 of those deaths can be blamed on just one tiger: **Champawat**, whose seven-year rampage at the turn of the 20th century **terrorized Nepal and India**. And though tiger populations are dwindling, attacks are still an issue in those areas.

This makes **the infamous tiger attack on Roy Horn**, of Siegfried & Roy, seem inevitable. Though the 400-pound white tiger went for Roy's throat, *he insists the tiger saved his life.* Roy claims he was already falling from a dizzy spell and the tiger tried to bring him to safety. But Ron Tilson, Minnesota Zoo's former director of conservation, had a different take: "When tigers kill prey and they want to move it out from the open into a more secure place, **they'll usually grab it by the neck.**"

CAT

According to at least one study published in a psychology journal, **cats are certifiably nuts**. The study compared the behavior of domestic cats to wild ones and found they're most similar to lions—both tend to be **dominant, impulsive and neurotic**. Of course, any cat owner could have told you that. They'd also say because cats weigh about 9 pounds, sleep 15 hours per day and sometimes fall off window sills, *their behavior is mostly adorable.*

More concerning are cat scratches, which can transmit bacteria that causes **cat-scratch disease**. According to the CDC, symptoms include fever, tender and enlarged lymph nodes, and pustules at the scratch site. Rarely, people also develop **eye infections, extreme muscle pain or even encephalitis, aka brain swelling** (*for those of you who aren't neurologists, brain swelling is bad*). Death is rare in those with healthy immune systems, but about 500 U.S. people are hospitalized for this each year.

LEOPARD

In his 1948 book *The Man-eating Leopard of Rudraprayag*, hunter Jim Corbett wrote that this beast was "not against the laws of nature, but against the laws of man." The leopard, **which killed at least 125 people over eight years** and was eventually killed by Corbett, was a prime example of some of nature's finest evolutionary feats.

Leopards are excellent at swimming and climbing, and though they're smaller than the rest of their big cat cousins, they make up for it with **stealth and adaptability**. They're the most geographically widespread of the big cats, thriving in deserts as well as rainforests, yet they're also the most difficult for humans to track and capture on film. *Basically, they're nature's perfect assassins.*

Though leopard attacks are relatively rare in most of the world, they're still fairly common in places like India. A study from 2016 suggested an average of 60 leopard attacks per year between 1998 and 2012 in the northern Indian state Uttarakhand—*that's more than once per week, which is a completely terrifying way to live.* As one local man told the newspaper *Indian Express*, "It's not just the attack from an animal. **It's the realization that you, your children, are just food.**"

HYENA

According to Gordon Grice, author of *The Book of Deadly Animals*, being eaten by a hyena is one of the worst ways you can go—it's not fast, and it's incredibly painful. In fact, he described it as "gruesome" when speaking with British newspaper the *Daily Mail*. **"They will maybe bite off a part of your face or another sensitive body part and just start eating you. This would be one of the worst deaths as it would be very long,"** explained Grice.

Unfortunately, ***having part of your face ripped off by a hyena is very possible in certain parts of the world***, especially Ethiopia's capital, Addis Ababa. There, "urban hyenas" are regularly seen lurking around in packs of up to 40. While they're great for culling the population of stray dogs and cats and eating any other animal carcasses that might be around (hyenas are famous for their bone-eating abilities), they also **dig up graves and eat human corpses** and, as mentioned earlier, ***attack the occasional live human face***.

WOLF

Wild wolf attacks are incredibly rare and almost never fatal, especially in modern-day North America. In fact, ***they're so uncommon that Minnesota's first documented wolf attack resulting in significant injury occurred in 2013***. In what was described by newspapers as a "freak accident," **a wolf bit the head of a 16-year-old** who was lying outside his tent in the campgrounds of Chippewa National Forest. (Thankfully, the boy was relatively unhurt.)

According to Dan Stark, a large carnivore specialist for Minnesota's Department of Natural Resources, this weird behavior meant the wolf was not well. The wolf was trapped and killed two days after the attack, and necropsy results showed **a facial deformity, abnormal teeth and brain damage** as a result of infection. As Stark put it, "Whether it actually knew what it was biting into is probably unlikely. It was biting something on the ground, ***and it happened to bite into somebody's head***."

GREAT WHITE SHARK

Though sharks are famous for being **exceptional killing machines with rows of serrated teeth and organs that can sense the electromagnetic fields of nearby animals**, whole humans aren't usually on the menu. According to the International Shark Attack File, a yearly report compiled by the Florida Museum, there were 66 "unprovoked" shark attacks and 34 "provoked" attacks around the world in 2018. **Only five of these attacks were fatal**.

If those numbers sound small, it's because they are. Sharks tend to go for smaller, more palatable prey and take "exploratory" bites out of humans instead of tearing them apart for food. *Still, "but he was just curious" isn't an excuse most people who've had a shark chomp off one of their limbs want to hear.*

Even though the chances of getting attacked by a shark are already pretty slim, you can protect yourself even further by never going surfing, as **about half of the shark attack victims in 2018 were surfing or participating in a similar board sport**. Apart from the fact that these sports naturally place people in the surf zone, the most frequent place for shark attacks, researchers think "**wiping out**" may be an activity that attracts sharks—*apparently, they're very judgmental about form.*

In 2006, 15-year-old Zac Golebiowski was surfing with his brother at Wharton Beach, a destination on Australia's southern coast favored for its sandbar breaks which create very shallow waters near the shore. As he told *The Guardian*: "The shark came in from deeper water and took my right leg…. When I take my friends to where the attack happened, they are always amazed that a shark attack could have happened there." Golebiowski still goes out on boogie boards, but not at Wharton—since his attack, there have been at least eight fatalities in the same area.

PUFFERFISH

For pufferfish, the best defense isn't a good offense—*it's just having an incredible defense*. These relatively small fish only grow up to 3 feet long, but they can seem much bigger when they want to by inflating themselves. **Using their weirdly elastic stomachs, pufferfish ingest large amounts of water to quickly puff themselves up and become an impossible-to-eat ball three times their normal size.** And oh, some kinds of pufferfish are covered in spines, making them even less appetizing.

If a predator does eat one of these fish before it manages to inflate itself, it will be sorry. Pufferfish contain **tetrodotoxin**, which is 1,200 times more poisonous than cyanide. Because of this, most creatures learn pretty quickly not to bother with pufferfish—*except humans, that is*....

Humans with adventurous appetites (and perhaps a death wish) regularly order *fugu*, a Japanese specialty of pufferfish meat. Only licensed and trained chefs are allowed to prepare the meal, as cutting it incorrectly means more than a very bad *Yelp* review—one pufferfish contains enough toxins to kill 30 adults. The first sign of poisoning is a feeling of numbness around the mouth. Soon after, the victim becomes paralyzed and will die from asphyxiation, thoroughly ruining everyone's dinner.

STRIPED SURGEONFISH

There are about 75 different species of surgeonfish, which are also known as **tang**. The brightly colored reef fish are so pretty that Pixar picked a blue tang for one of its most famously forgetful characters of all time, Dory. What Pixar neglected to mention, however, is that **you should never ever touch one of these fish**. (*This is actually pretty good advice regardless of the animal you're thinking of touching in the wild.*)

Named for the **scalpel-like blades** near the base of the spine that they can extend on command, *surgeonfish are basically multi-pronged pocket knives that just keep swimming*. But that's not the worst part—striped surgeonfish spines also carry **venom**.

Fortunately, like most sea creatures, surgeonfish will leave you alone as long as you extend them the same courtesy. Unfortunately, people love looking at these fish and they're very popular in aquariums, *making cleaning a treacherous task*.

NEEDLEFISH

If there's one place you don't expect a fish to attack from, it's the air. As far as scientists know, needlefish, also known as **Long Toms**, are the only fish to employ this method. Needlefish **launch themselves out of the water at up to 40 miles per hour** and dive back down to lunge at their prey with their long, tooth-lined jaws. *If this sounds baller to you, that's because it is*.

Despite the awesomeness of these aerial attacks, they lose some of their appeal when you're swimming or boating in Indo-Pacific waters and **get struck by a 6-inch-long needle that was hurtling along at the speed of a car**.

Multiple people have been stabbed and killed by needlefish. In 2014, one Russian tourist speared while swimming in Nha Trang, Vietnam, survived, but suffered **serious neck and spinal cord injuries** and was forced to endure **seven and a half hours of surgery** to remove multiple pieces of needlefish bone and teeth from her neck.

CASSOWARY

Regarded as the most dangerous birds on the planet, **cassowaries are the only feathered beasts* known to stab and kill humans**. These flightless birds are roughly human-sized, weighing up to 170 pounds and standing between 4 and 6 feet tall. Their most inhuman quality (*aside from being cold-blooded birds*) is their claws—cassowaries have **4-inch claws** on each of their feet, making their powerful kicks perfect for slicing up predators. Given that they also have a vertical jump of up to 7 feet, *these beady-eyed monsters should probably have their own horror film franchise.*

Most cassowary attacks occur when humans get too close or make a habit of feeding the birds, *as they are very territorial and prone to getting hangry.* According to *Scientific American*, "Serious injuries resulting from cassowary attacks are most likely to occur if the person is crouching or is lying or has fallen on the ground." This was borne out in 2019, when **a Florida man fell down and was attacked and killed by his pet cassowary**. People have also been scared by cassowaries attacking their doors and windows, but scientists say they're probably just attacking their own reflections.

*Technically, a man was also stabbed and killed by a rooster in 2011. But this happened at an illegal cockfight, and he was stabbed in the leg by a rooster with a knife attached to its leg, so we're calling *fowl* play.

SWAN

Swans are usually recognized for their grace and beauty, *but they should also be known for being total jerks*. Some properties even keep swans for this reason, as their territorial proclivities mean they keep away geese, *aka uglier jerks*. But like most bullies, swans have a tendency to take things too far.

According to John Huston, who works at the Abbotsbury Swannery in Dorset, swans are not dangerous—**in 600 years of the swannery's existence, there are no recorded attacks on humans**. As he told *BBC* in 2012, "They are not that strong and it's mostly show and bluster." Hurston also says he has never gotten more than a bruise from a swan.

But naturally, there are exceptions to every rule. In 2012, an Illinois man was kayaking when a swan knocked him into the water and caused the kayak to capsize. **The swan then blocked the man from swimming to shore, eventually causing him to drown**. *Talk about an ugly duckling.*

CANADA GOOSE

Humans are often safe from animals because they are just as fearful of us as we are of them. *This is not the case with Canada geese, which have learned humans will often run, cower and duck when attacked by a 13-pound bird*. Ironically, this happened because we didn't hunt Canada geese for a few decades after they became endangered, and many people even fed the birds instead. **This replenished their numbers, but came with the side effect of the occasional goose attack**.

The silver lining to this is that Canada geese, **lacking strength, sharp talons or the intelligence to attack as a flock**, simply aren't equipped to kill. Goose attacks have resulted in **broken bones and head trauma**, but these injuries are more often the result of people tripping and falling during the assault. The takeaway? *Give geese a wide berth—and for the good of our species, stop feeding them.*

GIANT ANTEATER

Most people would be forgiven for assuming giant anteaters are pretty harmless—they **lack teeth, have poor eyesight and don't hear very well**, not to mention they spend most of their day moseying around and looking for ant hills to slurp on with their super-long tongues. (***Fun fact: Proportionally speaking, giant anteaters have the longest tongues of any mammal.***) But like most wild creatures, they're very territorial when threatened, **and you don't want to underestimate a giant anteater**.

Growing up to 7 feet long, they're known to stand on their hind legs when threatened, a position called the "**anteater's hug**." It is not wise to return an anteater's hug, *as you probably would have guessed upon noticing their sharp claws*.

Though giant anteater attacks are rare, they do occur when people encroach their territory, and **wounds from "ant bears" can be fatal**—at least two Brazilian hunters have died after run-ins with these freakishly long-tongued mammals.

SQUIRREL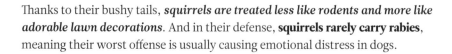

Thanks to their bushy tails, *squirrels are treated less like rodents and more like adorable lawn decorations*. And in their defense, **squirrels rarely carry rabies**, meaning their worst offense is usually causing emotional distress in dogs.

But sometimes, squirrels do go rogue. In 2016, a Florida squirrel infiltrated a retirement home and **bit and scratched multiple residents**, and in 2015 a San Francisco squirrel attacked an elderly couple in their garage, **bloodying the 87-year-old man's head, arms and legs**.

Squirrels may also get used to being fed by humans, leading them to *lash out when their nut supply runs dry*—this was a problem at Indiana University–Purdue University Indianapolis in 2017, when **multiple meal plan–dependent squirrels were biting students' ankles**.

SLOW LORIS

Weighing less than 3 pounds, these giant-eyed, cute little furballs have become internet sensations, leading some people to try to obtain them as pets simply for the 'Gram. As usual, *this is dumb for a few reasons*. First, **the slow loris is a wild nocturnal animal** and it would be cruel to keep one penned up. Second, these creatures are already near extinction, and the biggest threat to their species is the illegal animal trade. But third—*and perhaps most important if you value your life*—**is that as one of the few venomous mammals on the planet, a slow loris can kill you**.

Slow lorises have the unique feature of **venomous glands on their upper arms**. If one feels threatened by a predator (*or by a creature 75 times its size shoving an iPhone in its face*), the slow loris will lick those glands, mixing the venom with its saliva to create a toxic, extra-deadly bite.

Anna Nekaris, a conservation biologist at Oxford Brookes University, says **slow lorises between 1 and 2 years old are the most aggressive**. "The young ones, they really try to kill you," Nekaris told *National Geographic*. "They are incredibly strong. Some of them scream." Ah yes, the perfect cuddly pet—*a screaming ball of like-bait that's hell-bent on your destruction*. #SlowLorisMoreLikeNoLoris

BOX JELLYFISH

The most toxic animal on Earth isn't a snake, scorpion or your middle-school frenemy—it's the box jellyfish. You should be on the lookout for them if you're ever in the Indo-Pacific, where most horrifying sea creatures apparently like to hang out. **Armed (or rather, tentacled) with thousands of stinging cells, each one of these invertebrates carries enough venom to kill more than 60 humans**.

While getting stung by one of these jellyfish isn't a guaranteed death (there's a chance you might just be in extreme pain for a few weeks), according to *National Geographic*, the stings are so "overpoweringly painful, **human victims have been known to go into shock and drown or die of heart failure before even reaching shore**." Stings can also cause tissue necrosis and cardiac arrest—*all in all, it's a pretty powerful move for a creature that mostly looks like a plastic grocery bag.*

Currently, **there is no antidote for box jellyfish venom**, but that might not be true for long. Researchers at the University of Sydney say they have discovered a potential antidote for the venom, which is great news, assuming victims don't die before they can get back to shore for treatment. But until this antidote becomes available, Queensland Ambulance Service suggests dousing the wounds with vinegar for at least 30 seconds to alleviate the pain, or try rinsing the wound with saltwater. **Do not urinate on a jellyfish sting— the idea that this alleviates the pain is a myth,** *probably made up by someone's middle-school frenemy.*

SMACK ATTACK

In 1997, Alaskan-born Angel Yanagihara was working on her doctorate researching cellular ion channels at the University of Hawaii. One early morning, she had gone out for a predawn swim when she suddenly found herself in the middle of a group (aka a smack) of jellyfish—the translucent creatures are already difficult to see underwater and essentially invisible in low light. As described in 2018 in the journal *Science*, "she felt needles burning into her neck and arms and her lungs collapsing; her arms began to fail." Using breathing techniques she had learned in birthing classes to fight through the pain, Yanagihara managed to drag herself to shore and recovered after spending three days in the hospital. Determined to understand more about what almost killed her, Yanagihara now researches box jellyfish and is working to develop sting treatments.

DEER

If you live in America, **the animal you're most likely to be killed by isn't a cougar, bear or snake: It's a deer**. If you're thinking deer don't attack people, you're mostly right, though there are very rare examples of deer fighting back against hunters. One such case was the Louisiana man who shot a deer on his property in 2014, **only to have the wounded animal use its antlers to gore his thigh, causing him to nearly bleed to death**.

But overall, *deer are much more deadly when their bodies inadvertently transform into pop-up roadblocks*, an unfortunate habit that causes car accidents and **kills around 120 people per year**. In deer's defense, they can't help it—they're **crepuscular** animals, meaning they are most active at dusk and dawn, and have their pupils fully dilated to take in as much light as possible. So when deer wander into roads and see headlights, they do get literally stuck—**the light blinds them and they stay still until their eyes can adjust**. *Unfortunately, they're usually roadkill before this can happen.*

COUGAR TOWN

Some experts have suggested rejuvenating the cougar population to help keep the deer population in check. Don't worry—according to a 2011 paper in *Human-Wildlife Interactions*, "Relative to other large carnivores with a history of attacking humans, cougars are among the least lethal."

HORSE

Most horse-related deaths are accidents—**getting kicked in the head, bucked off a spooked horse or being unintentionally trampled are all terrifying potential side effects of riding horses**, though there's a small amount of comfort to be taken in the idea that the horse wasn't actually trying to murder you.

However, there are instances of horses **literally being out for blood**. In 2017, a Houston man named Ivory Lindsey was returning his horse to its stable when the horse in the next stall attacked without warning, *biting the man's throat as if it were a carrot*. "**I reached to grab my throat and I didn't,**" Lindsey told ABC. "I got scared because I knew he had pulled it out."

Incredibly, Lindsey's life was saved after he was rushed to the hospital and had surgery to reconstruct his throat. He learned to speak again (*though he is presumably a little hoarse*).

DOG

Because people think of their pets as family, dog attacks can be **even more alarming** than wild-animal attacks—the sense of betrayal stings, *almost as much as the tetanus shot you probably need*. Of course, people treating dogs like children is one of the main reasons dogs bite.

One report estimated **dogs bite more than 4 million people in the U.S. each year**, with up to 13,000 of those incidents requiring hospital treatment. And while just a tiny fraction of those incidents result in death—an average of 19 per year—*those incidents can be especially grisly*.

In 2019, Nancy Burgess-Dismuke was playing with her two boxer mixes on her lawn when they became violent. Denzel Whiteside, a neighbor who helped fend the dogs off, explained her injuries: "**One arm was already bit completely off, the other arm was barely hanging on by a piece of meat.**" Tragically, she lost too much blood and did not survive the attack.

ATLANTIC BLUEFIN TUNA

Though they grow to about 6.5 feet long and usually weigh around 550 pounds (and can weigh a lot more), the Atlantic bluefin tuna isn't much of a threat to humans—*at least not while they're still alive and swimming around.* Ironically, **tuna becomes a lot more dangerous once it's butchered and served to you,** whether from a can or in a sushi roll.

You guessed it—we're talking about mercury poisoning. Mercury is a naturally occurring element, and a highly toxic form of mercury called methylmercury can build up in fish, shellfish and the animals that eat those fish, like humans. You can safely ingest moderate amounts of methylmercury, but packing a tuna sandwich for your daily lunch isn't a good idea—especially if you're pregnant or happen to be a small child.

Signs of methylmercury poisoning include "pins and needles" feelings; loss of coordination; speech, peripheral vision, hearing and walking impairment; and muscle weakness. If that isn't bad enough, unborn children are much more vulnerable to methylmercury poisoning—it can potentially affect their cognitive thinking, memory, language, fine motor skills and visual spatial skills.

Note: This is slightly different from **metallic mercury poisoning**, which happens when you breathe in mercury vapors. Read more about that nightmare on page 230.

STINGRAY

Stingrays aren't usually much of a threat to humans: They keep to themselves, spend most of their time half-buried in sand and mostly eat mollusks. But their **sharp, sometimes venomous spines** can be deadly.

Also known as a barb, a stingray's tail is its only defense, but it's a pretty good one. If a human steps on a smaller stingray, **they'll likely be alerted by the sharp sting of the barb on their foot or ankle**, an outcome that is painful but not deadly. But in larger stingrays, which can weigh up to 790 pounds, **the barb can even be a solid defense against a shark**.

Most human-stingray encounters aren't deadly—the venom won't kill unless it hits you in the chest. If you do get stung by a stingray, **channel Captain John Smith**, who almost died from a stingray wound. Allegedly, a doctor saved him after applying heat to the wound (an effective method of breaking down their venom) *and Smith ate the stingray for dinner.*

CONE SNAIL

Armored in a beautiful brown, black and white patterned shell, cone snails evoke the look of an overpriced paperweight from Anthropologie. But hiding underneath that trendy exterior is a **tiny snail assassin**.

A cone snail kills its prey with a venomous sting, delivered by a proboscis from its mouth. The proboscis is super sharp, making it easy to penetrate a fish's tough outer skin—*or an unsuspecting diver's gloves.*

The extra-terrifying part is you might not have any idea you've been stung. Because their venom has pain-killing properties, **you may not realize you've been poisoned until it's far too late**. When you do begin to notice symptoms, they may include intense pain, tingling and numbness, or in more severe cases, muscle paralysis, blurred or double vision and respiratory paralysis—*which adds up to a generally bad, fatal time.*

DOLPHINS

Though we mostly think of dolphins as cute and playful sea mammals, they're shockingly cruel to other animals and even to each other. Male dolphins have been seen **attacking baby porpoises for no apparent reason**, relentlessly batting them around until they die. Groups of males have also been known to force females to mate with them for weeks—*you probably fell asleep during those scenes in* Flipper.

But, perhaps out of sheer pity—their sense of echolocation allows them to tell when our hearts are beating out of our chests—dolphins have historically been kind to humans, saving them from drowning or becoming shark food. But not all dolphins are willing to babysit us, especially when humans push them too far.

In 1994, a dolphin nicknamed **Tião** was a frequent visitor to Caraguatatuba, a beach on Brazil's southern coast. **People would crowd the dolphin, try to ride it, tie objects to its tail and even tried to shove ice cream in his blowhole,** *which had the not-shocking effect of pissing Tião right off.* The dolphin lashed out, minorly injuring 29 swimmers and majorly injuring one man, **who later died from internal bleeding**.

LEOPARD SEAL

Growing up to 11.5 feet and weighing around 800 pounds, **leopard seals are aggressive hunters famous for taking down larger prey**, like other seals. They also enjoy picking off penguins as they dive into the water. According to *National Geographic*: **"The captured bird is thrashed about on the water until its skin peels away**. The remaining carcass is then eaten." *Ah, the circle of life.*

Leopard seals also like to attack inflatable boats, but otherwise don't pose much of a threat to humans—still, **this is probably only because humans generally aren't in the Antarctic, where leopard seals live in the wild**.

In 1985, polar explorer Gareth Wood experienced what must have been the fright of his life when a leopard seal burst through the thin layer of ice he was walking on. As he later wrote about the encounter: "Suddenly, the surface erupted as the massive head and shoulders of a mature leopard seal, mouth gaping in expectation, crashed through the eggshell covering. It closed its powerful jaws around my right leg and I fell backward, shocked and helpless." Luckily for him, his companions got the seal to let go by repeatedly kicking it with their ice crampons, aka those pointy ice shoes.

STONEFISH

Cleverly named for their resemblance to a rock, stonefish spend the majority of their time seamlessly blending in with coral and rocky reefs, waiting for an unsuspecting reef fish to get too close so they can swallow it whole. Because stonefish are just 1 to 2 feet in size, humans don't have to worry about being swallowed. But people should still be wary, **as accidentally stepping on a stonefish can be deadly**.

Equipped with **13 venom-filled spines along their backs**, stonefish are well-protected from pretty much any ocean predator, including humans. The **excruciatingly painful venom can kill a person in under an hour,** so if you're ever swimming in waters off the northern Australian coast, you'd be wise to wear sturdy water shoes.

If you are pierced by the venomous spine of a stonefish, you can expect immediate, agonizing pain, muscle paralysis, difficulty breathing, shock and potential heart failure and death—all in all, not a pleasant way to go. On the bright side, scientists have developed an antivenom for stonefish stings, *so you might make it if you get treatment quickly.*

NONTOXIC NOMS

If you're feeling daring, you can enjoy a meal of cooked or raw stonefish—apparently, it's delicious. After removing the toxic dorsal fin, the rest of the fish meat is safe to eat.

Around 2003, scientists noticed another insane evolutionary feat in stonefish—their ability to flick out an extra blade-like bone from their faces. Technically referred to as a "lachrymal saber," stonefish can use their cheek muscles to deploy this extra defense whenever they want, though scientists still aren't sure whether the fluorescent green, nontoxic protrusion is used for defense or in courtship behaviors. The Wolverine-esque ability was first noticed by William Leo Smith, associate curator and associate professor of ecology and evolutionary biology at the University of Kansas. Among many more scientific-sounding questions he had about the discovery was this: "Why do we see this accumulation of so many horrible things on one fish?"

KOMODO DRAGON

Komodo dragons weigh up to 200 pounds, reach lengths of about 8.5 feet and will eat pretty much anything, *including you*. Worst of all, their saliva is full of bacteria and venom. **So if one bites you, you're in for a slow death.**

After biting you, the dragon will wait a few days for you to die, then eat pretty much all of you— **they can eat up to 80 percent of their body weight in one sitting**.

Komodo dragon attacks are rare, as they are native to five Indonesian islands. *But your odds worsen if you purposefully decide to hang out with one.* In 2001, Sharon Stone arranged for her then-husband, Phil Bronstein, to visit a dragon at the L.A. Zoo. As Stone recalled, the zoo encouraged him to pet the reptile, **which predictably ended with the dragon lunging and biting his foot**. "Phil screamed and we heard this crunching sound," said Stone. Bronstein lived, but their marriage died three years later.

INLAND TAIPAN SNAKE

As a snake that feeds almost entirely on mammals, inland taipan snakes have developed venom that is extra potent on warm-blooded prey. *And if you didn't know, that group includes humans.* Neurotoxins from taipan venom can result in **slurred speech, seizures and breathing difficulties**. It also has hemotoxins which can lead to internal bleeding and organ damage—**victims can die in as little as 45 minutes**.

According to David Penning, *a biologist and snake expert/ apologist at the Missouri Southern State University*, **people should be very safe from taipans as long as they resist the urge to touch them**. In Penning's experience, people only get bitten when they try to handle the snake. "I have yet to read a news story about someone being bitten by a snake they didn't know was there," said Penning in 2017.

NILE MONITOR LIZARD

Nile monitor lizards are native to Africa, *but thanks to some Floridians with very questionable taste in pets*, they're now found in the Sunshine State as well. Monitors can wander very far, grow and breed relatively quickly and lay up to 60 eggs per clutch, all of which means **their populations have grown into the thousands since the first one was spotted in Florida in 1990.** Today, if you see a monitor lizard or any other invasive species in Florida, you can report it to the IveGot1 app or *IveGot1.org* (*we're not kidding; that's the name*).

Wildly, some people still think it's a good idea to keep a 6-foot long lizard that has no qualms about eating you as a pet. One such person was Ronald Huff, who kept seven Nile monitors in his Delaware apartment. In 2002, Huff was found dead in his apartment, half-eaten by these ravenous reptiles.

In a gruesome 2018 article from *The Sun*, Huff's neighbor recalled the scene: "**The blood had just all turned black; it looked like fake blood. His cheeks had been eaten off and his molars were where his ears should be. They had eaten his face, eaten his hands, they actually had eaten into his abdomen and eaten some of the internal organs**." His neighbor claimed Huff had died earlier from an infected bite, not from a direct attack, but coroners ruled this inconclusive.

COMMON DEATH ADDER

These relatively short snakes top out at about 3 feet long, but this suits them. Unlike other snakes, which depend on their length for speed and agility, **death adders prefer to hunt via ambush**. The snake blends in with the ground and waits for days until a small mammal, bird or human ankle happens to wander by, then uses its short, muscular body to quickly strike at unsuspecting prey.

Unsurprisingly, death adders are very venomous. However, you might get lucky if one bites you. Because their venom is very precious to them, as it takes a lot of energy to produce, *you might get off with just a warning bite if they deem you to be a low-level threat.* This could hurt your pride, but the venom would hurt a lot worse—you'll experience symptoms such as **abdominal pain, headaches, drowsiness, swelling of the lymph nodes and asphyxiation**. If no one's around to help you breathe, you'll die.

SPITTING COBRA

If you're looking for another reason to be both impressed and petrified by Mother Nature, we present to you the spitting cobra. Unlike most venomous snakes, which need to bite you to inject venom, **spitting cobras can spray venom at you through their fangs from up to 6 feet away and more than 40 times in rapid succession**.

Their venom won't hurt you if it hits your skin or even the insides of your mouth, but if it gets in your eyes, **it will cause incredible amounts of pain and potentially scar your corneas and blind you**. Also, if a spitting cobra has you in its crosshairs, it probably will hit you in at least one eye—**the snakes are crack shots, hitting a target's eyes 80 to 100 percent of the time** in a 2005 study by the University of Bonn in Germany. (*Note: The targets were photos of faces and the face of an undergraduate student named Katja Tzschätzsch.*)

You should also be wary of the fact that spitting cobras can still inject you with venom via biting. In fact, they can even do this if you chop off their heads. This happened to Chinese chef Peng Fan in 2014, who had been preparing a spitting cobra for a special soup. When he tried to throw out the snake's head, it reflexively bit him. There is an antivenom for spitting cobras, but sadly Peng died before it could be administered.

PYTHON

Growing up to 25 feet long, **pythons have the mind-boggling distinction of being able to kill people in one of the most horrifying ways imaginable while still being allowed to dwell in our homes as pets**. In fact, if you have a few hundred dollars, you can pretty easily procure a giant snake that wants to squeeze you to death and then swallow you whole. *What a time to be alive! And then dead.*

Larger pythons have no trouble taking down prey that is much stronger than the average human. (*If you want to see this in action, look up the absolutely bonkers video of a python eating an alligator.*) After they use their sharp teeth to latch onto a victim, **they wrap their bodies around their prey and squeeze, causing suffocation**. Then, the python can take its time in utilizing its stretchy jaw ligaments to swallow the animal whole.

And it's not just the big boys that can end a man's life. Even relatively shorter pythons are capable of killing humans. **In 1996, a 13-foot python killed its teenage owner in their Bronx apartment**. According to *The New York Times*, the 19-year-old was found "**lying face down in a pool of blood in the hallway of his apartment building with the snake coiled around his midriff and back**." The python had been bought at a local store five months earlier for just $300.

Wild python attacks are extremely rare, but according to David Penning, an assistant professor of biology at Missouri Southern State University, they may be increasing as humans cut down their habitats, forcing more interactions between us and them. In 2018, a 23-foot python killed a woman in central Indonesia. The victim, 54-year-old Wa Tiba, went missing after leaving to check on her garden one evening. When her family and other villagers went to look for her the next day, they found her sandals, a flashlight and, about 165 feet away, a bloated snake. According to the village's chief: "When they cut open the snake's belly, they found Tiba's body still intact with all her clothes. She was swallowed first from her head."

ANACONDA

As the python's South American cousin, anacondas have a very similar modus operandi. Both creatures squeeze and suffocate their prey then stretch their jaws open to swallow it whole. **And like pythons, anacondas can digest anything with enough time.** Green anacondas, the largest of the species (and the heaviest snakes in the world) regularly eat wild pigs, turtles and even jaguars—**the semiaquatic snakes like to lie in wait near the water's edge, then ambush whatever animal is unlucky enough to get too close.**

If you do ever see an anaconda, your best bet is to run. These snakes are incredibly stealthy in water, but pretty slow on land, and you'd be advised to get as far away as possible before it can wrap itself around you. A friend who really loves you may be able to uncoil the snake from your body—in 2007, a 66-year-old Brazilian man saved his grandson after spending a half hour uncoiling a 16-foot anaconda from his body—but if you're alone, you're probably screwed.

If you somehow manage to not suffocate when the anaconda squeezes you, you'll probably wish you did. **The angle of the snake's teeth make it difficult for any still-living prey to escape once the swallowing starts,** *and we're guessing you wouldn't be able to put up a better fight than a jaguar.*

44

SAW-SCALED VIPER

A wary saw-scaled viper will loop itself into S-shaped folds and move slowly, causing its scales to rub together and create a hissing sound that serves as a warning for any nearby predators or bumbling humans. **Though this small snake only grows up to about 20 inches, it should send shivers down your spine if you ever see or hear one**.

Most venomous snakes prefer to save their venom for the most serious threats, conserving their lethality for emergencies. *The saw-scaled viper, on the other hand, is all HAM all the time, preferring to unload all its venom on its first strike*. This approach is largely why they're believed to be more deadly than the rest of the snakes in the same regions combined. And that's a lot of regions—**saw-scaled vipers are found in dry savannas in northern Africa, parts of the Middle East and Central Asia**.

If you are bitten by a saw-scaled viper, prepare to lose your life or at least a limb. According to *National Geographic*, the saw-scaled viper's venom "doesn't just kill, it *destroys*." *Nat Geo* backs up this dramatic statement with a vividly disgusting description of one 13-year-old's bite: "The boy's hand swelled up and his skin turned white. He started bleeding from huge open gashes in his knuckles and arms. Worse still, the flesh in his hand started rotting." Apparently, on top of devastating your skin tissue, the viper's venom destroys the membranes in your blood vessels, making it impossible for your blood to clot, which in turn causes "catastrophic bleeding," a phrase no one wants to have associated with their bodies.

DEATHSTALKER SCORPION

Small enough to seem like it may not cause that much damage (*but too big to trap under your average mug*), the deathstalker scorpion is basically **a 4-inch venom syringe** that's ready to inject you if you breathe in its general direction.

You would think the deathstalker, **which has the strongest venom of any scorpion**, would look a little more threatening. *But don't be fooled by its fragile-looking baby pincers*: its venom is so strong, this scorpion simply doesn't need them. It just needs to sting quickly, which it does—**the deathstalker scorpion can whip its tail 51 inches per second, delivering a hell of a sting**.

MILK MONEY

This scorpion's venom is the most expensive liquid in the world. It is valued at $39 million per gallon, but you'd need to milk one scorpion 2.64 million times to get that much. Sounds crazy, but the medical community thinks it's worth it for developing new medicines.

Deathstalker stings are, as you've probably surmised, rather unpleasant. **The venom in their sting causes all your muscles to contract at once, resulting in paralysis**. If you're a bug, that gives the scorpion plenty of time to eat you. If you're a human, you're a bit large for the scorpion's appetite, *but you might die anyway*. According to New York–Presbyterian Hospital, their sting produces **extreme pain, convulsions, the aforementioned paralysis, and death from heart and respiratory failure**.

GOLDEN POISON FROG

If you have a hard time not picking up cute and colorful frogs that are under 2 inches long (*seriously,* **Nat Geo** *compares this adorable amphibian to a paperclip*), then you should never visit the South American rainforests, the home of these **impossibly poisonous frogs**. You're dead meat as soon as you touch a golden poison frog, as their skin is totally toxic. In Colombia, the indigenous Emberá people put this to good use, using the frogs' poison to tip their blowgun darts—hence the nickname of poison dart frogs.

D.I.Y. DARTS

Here's something for your Pinterest board: According to an account published in 1978, extracting poison from these frogs was a cruel but effective process. After trapping the frog, people would "pass a pointed piece of wood down his throat and out at one of his legs." This would make the frog sweat poison. Darts dipped in poisonous frog sweat stayed extra deadly for one year.

Not all species of poison frogs are toxic enough to kill someone, but this bright yellow frog certainly is—**their skin has enough poison to kill 10 people**. This makes for an excellent defense for an otherwise helpless creature; only snakes resistant to their poison prey on them. **Nonresistant predators, including humans, instead experience the very adverse effects of paralysis and death**.

BRAZILIAN WANDERING SPIDER

Dangerous to humans and each other (*females have a thing for attacking their mates once they're done, well, mating*), Brazilian wandering spiders got their name for their ambulatory habits. Instead of building webs, **these arachnids hide during the day and wander the forest floor at night, looking for their next meal to attack or ambush**. According to Jo-Anne Nina Sewlal, an arachnologist at the University of the West Indies in Trinidad, a bite from a Brazilian wandering spider isn't predatory, but rather "**a means of self-defense and only done if they are provoked intentionally or by accident**."

Of course, people who get a large dose of venom from these spiders probably don't particularly care that it was in self-defense, as they're too busy dealing with severe burning pain, sweating and goose bumps. Within a half hour, they'll have many more symptoms to deal with, **including nausea, abdominal cramping, hypothermia, high or low blood pressure, a fast or slow heartbeat, blurred vision and convulsions**.

Men are also vulnerable to one more side effect—**painful erections that last for hours**. This is a result of the venom increasing nitric oxide, which increases blood flow. (*In other news, studies have looked into using the venom in certain drugs targeted at men.*) On the plus side, bites containing enough venom to bring on most of these side effects are rare—**as of 2008, only 10 deaths in Brazil had been attributed to this spider**.

In 2014, a British family found a venomous addition to their grocery delivery: one Brazilian wandering spider in a bunch of bananas, guarding its sac containing thousands of eggs. In a hilarious-but-only-because-no-one-died turn of events, the shocked father of the family dropped the bananas into a fruit bowl, trapping the spider's leg. Determined not to be pinned down, the spider tore off its leg, ran and hid, causing the family to run from their own home. Eventually, a pest control expert was called in and successfully removed the spider and egg sac. According to *The Guardian*, this was the second time in a year that one of these deadly spiders had entered the U.K. via banana.

SIX-EYED SAND SPIDER

Native to the deserts of southern Africa, **six-eyed sand spiders are both extremely venomous and extraordinarily good at hide-and-seek**. Because they're covered in tiny hairs known as setae, these spiders can basically wear a coat of sand at all times—*a very convenient trait to have when you're trying to blend in with the desert.* For 100 percent camouflage, the six-eyed sand spider will completely bury itself under the sand, where it then waits to ambush scorpions or insects that happen to pass by.

While this spider is super-shy, it's also, as previously mentioned, super-deadly. **If you accidentally got too close, their bite would probably kill you**. Sand spider venom has both haemolytic and necrotic effects, *which are fancy science words meaning your blood vessels would start to leak and your tissues would break down.* And to make matters worse, scientists have not yet developed an antivenom for this spider.

Sand spiders are so reluctant to bite people, however, that there are no confirmed bites and only two suspected bites. Whatever got the victims of the suspected bites was pretty gnarly: one person lost an arm to extreme necrosis and the other died from blood hemorrhaging, aka profuse bleeding from leaky blood vessels.

BROWN RECLUSE SPIDER

Found mostly in the southeastern U.S., *these spiders seem like they've been designed to give you the creeps.* The tiny venomous spiders like to hide in man-made spaces, such as your closet, under your porch or inside your shoes.

These spiders also have a weird biological hack: **As long as a female mates just once, she'll produce eggs forever.** This means a lone female spider can infest your home with 150 more spiderlings, *starting a cycle that ends with you burning your house down,* Arachnophobia-style.

Getting bitten by a brown recluse is like playing Russian roulette: some people with low sensitivity may have no reaction at all, while others may experience **necrotic arachnidism,** aka tissue death via spider bite, and severe reactions can result in what's called a "volcano lesion." **This means the tissue becomes gangrenous and develops into an open wound roughly the size of your hand,** *which is generally not a good look.*

SYDNEY FUNNEL-WEB SPIDER

Like the majority of Australia's dangerous creatures, Sydney funnel-web spiders can kill you in under 15 minutes. These venomous spiders have **backward-facing fangs sharp enough to go through your fingernail,** which would actually be a good place to get bitten—you'll want a tourniquet applied, stat. According to Dr. Robert Raven, curator of arachnids at Queensland Museum, **"The most dangerous place to get bitten is the torso because no tourniquet can be put on it."**

If you are bitten by this spider, you'll know it immediately. Thanks to an evolutionary quirk, **their venom has severe effects on primates' nervous systems, causing symptoms such as rapid heart rate, numbness around the mouth and difficulty breathing.** But while their venom paralyzes invertebrates (the spider's main food source) and makes our nervous systems go haywire, most Australian pets can rest easy—**according to Raven, cats and dogs can neutralize the toxin in about a half hour.**

KISSING BUG

Technically named **triatomine bugs**, *kissing bugs got their moniker for behaving like tiny, deranged Prince Charmings—instead of kissing, they bite sleeping people near their lips.* This happens for a few reasons: kissing bugs are nocturnal, they're looking for blood to slurp on, they're attracted to the carbon dioxide you're breathing out **and a person's face is often the only exposed part of their body while sleeping**.

If you thought an insect biting you on the face is the worst thing it can do to you while you slumber, allow us to further fuel your nightmares. Kissing bugs also carry **parasites**, but they aren't transmitted through biting—**they're transmitted through their poop and, naturally, the bug defecates right after it bites you**. According to the CDC, people usually get infected after they accidentally rub the poop into their eyes, mouth or a wound. *So if you get bit and then rub your face when you wake up, congratulations!* **You have a 33 percent chance of getting chronic Chagas disease**.

Caused by that parasite the kissing bug pooped onto your face (*Trypanosoma cruzi*), **chronic Chagas disease can cause a stiff heart that is bad at pumping blood, an enlarged esophagus or colon that can make it hard to eat or go No. 2, and heart rhythm problems that can suddenly kill you**.

> ### BUG BITES
> The bite itself won't hurt, but according to Texas A&M University, "Reactions to kissing bug bites have been reported to vary from unnoticeable to anaphylactic shock."

In case climate change wasn't bad enough, a warmer planet means more places these bugs can thrive. The kissing bug has historically preferred the warmer climates of South America, Central America, Mexico and the southern U.S., but in recent years they seem to have been crawling north. In 2018, a young girl in Delaware was bitten by a kissing bug that had made its way into her bedroom.

Research from Texas A&M University has found more than 50 percent of kissing bugs are carriers of the parasite that causes Chagas disease, but this bug was not one of them.

BULLET ANT

Technically, a sting (or even multiple stings) from a bullet ant won't kill you. *But if you're stung by one, you'll probably wish you were dead.* **So named because their sting feels like getting shot by a gun, the bullet ant has the most painful sting of any insect.** And once you've been stung once, you're likely to be stung a few more times—the first bug to sting you releases a chemical that alerts any other ants nearby to sting you too.

Bullet ants do an incredible amount of damage with just one sting. On top of **electric, blinding pain that ebbs and flows for 12 to 24 hours**, venom from a bullet ant can also induce temporary paralysis, uncontrollable shaking, nausea, fever, vomiting and cardiac arrhythmia. *But hey, at least it's not lethal!*

Most people would do anything to avoid getting stung by one of these ants—but the men of the Sateré-Mawé tribe in Brazil are not most people. In a ritual that seems to be the literal definition of toxic masculinity, all boys of the tribe must wear a glove made of leaves and sedated bullet ants for five full minutes, inciting hundreds of ant stings. Once the boy undergoes this ritual 20 times, he will be accepted by the tribe as a man. Evidently, this prepares boys for all the dangers of the Amazon jungle. #hardpass.

ASIAN GIANT HORNET

These freakishly large hornets, found mostly in rural Japan, southeast Asia and occasionally North America, like to spend their time utterly devastating colonies of smaller honeybees. **A small group of hornets will go in and begin ripping off the smaller bees' heads, and can wipe out a colony of 30,000 in a matter of hours**. *Then, the honey and larvae are theirs for the pillaging.*

On top of being much larger than the average honeybee—**giant hornets are about 2 inches long**—they also have the advantage of stingers that aren't barbed. This means they can sting multiple times without leaving the stinger behind in their victim. **This is bad news for humans, as the giant hornet's stinger is sharp enough to pierce through some fabrics and is full of venom capable of destroying your flesh and overloading your kidneys**.

If you do see a hornet the size of your thumb, your best bet is to stay calm and still and hope it ignores you, as their stings can be deadly if not treated quickly enough. In 2013, an outbreak of giant hornets in northern China led to about 1,600 injuries and at least 42 deaths.

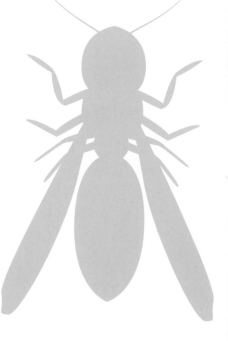

BEE

While bees are more than a little pesky, they're not usually deadly. Unless you're allergic to bee stings, doctors' orders usually involve a cold compress and a painkiller. *Or you can try just not being a baby for the next few hours until the swelling and pain subsides.* If you are severely allergic, however, bees can pose a real threat (we still see you, little Macaulay Culkin from *My Girl*). Victims can go into anaphylaxis, which includes **difficulty breathing; a weak, rapid pulse; nausea, vomiting or diarrhea; dizziness or fainting; and loss of consciousness.**

Of course, **you don't need to be allergic to be in danger if you're attacked by a literal swarm of bees.** Though this scenario is rare, it has happened. In 2016, 23-year-old Alex Bestler was hiking through Usery Mountain Park in Arizona when a large group of hostile bees began stinging him, **resulting in more than 1,000 stings.** Though people tried to help Bestler, who had fallen to the ground and was still covered in bees, the swarm kept them at bay.

Eventually a park sergeant was able to get close with a utility vehicle and pick up Bestler, **who was still covered with bees.** Unfortunately, Bestler was pronounced dead upon arrival at a local hospital.

SWEAT BEE

While most bees are all about getting that honey, these bees also want to drink your sweat and tears (but thankfully, not your blood). Technically called *Halictidae*, they're smaller than your usual bumblebee and about as dangerous; their stings shouldn't cause much alarm unless you're allergic. But because they also love to literally drink your protein-packed tears, they can cause a lot of psychological damage and, in a worst-case scenario, blindness.

In 2019, a woman from Taiwan experienced what probably seemed like a waking nightmare when her ophthalmologist pulled four live sweat bees from under her eyelid. The woman, who had gone for a hike the day before, had no idea bees were the cause of her persistent eye pain—initially, she assumed dirt had blown into her eyes.

SWEET SODIUM

Researchers think sweat bees are extra-attracted to human sweat because of our high sodium intake—apparently, they enjoy your french fries just as much as you do.

Later, Dr. Hong Chi Ting of the Fooyin University Hospital said it was **extremely lucky that the woman refrained from rubbing her eyes**. "She was wearing contact lenses so she didn't dare to rub her eyes in case she broke the lens. **If she did, she could have induced the bees to produce venom…. She could have gone blind.**"

MOSQUITO

In most of the western world, these tiny invertebrates are usually regarded as annoying for giving you itchy welts and keeping you awake by buzzing around your face. You can thank females in particular for the bites—**they're the only ones with the necessary proboscis for getting at your blood, which they need as a source of protein for their eggs**.

However, mosquitoes aren't just irritating: They're actually the deadliest animals on the planet. According to the World Health Organization, mosquitoes kill millions of people each year by spreading disease, with children and the elderly disproportionately affected. What's worse, scientists believe global warming is only going to make these disease demons even more widespread.

More than 3,000 species of mosquitoes exist, *but just three species are at assassin-like levels when it comes to killing humans*. Malaria, elephantiasis and encephalitis (inflammation of the brain) are carried by *Anopheles* mosquitoes; *Culex* mosquitoes carry encephalitis, elephantiasis and West Nile virus (page 181); and *Aedes* mosquitoes carry yellow fever (page 163), dengue (page 153) and also encephalitis.

When it comes to mosquitoes, **the CDC suggests you not get bitten in the first place**. Their site is full of useful tips such as using insect repellent, wearing long-sleeve shirts and pants and putting screens in your windows. *They also suggest a good way to avoid getting stabbed is to not shove a knife into your arm.*

If you thought disease-carrying mosquitoes were only found in Africa or South America, think again. Mosquitoes carrying West Nile virus are also common in the U.S., though less than 1 percent of people who are bitten contract a life-threatening form of the virus. Most people have no reactions at all, and about 20 percent of people only experience a fever and other light symptoms; there's a chance you've had it and brushed it off as the summer flu. But when the disease does strike, it's terrifying—in 2019, a Delaware woman named Janice Thurrell was nearly comatose for two months after contracting West Nile, presumably from a mosquito. She survived the ordeal, though as her husband said, "Once you get the symptoms, it's usually too late."

PERILOUS PARASITES

The world is filled with microscopic murderers. Gas-station sushi could lead to a take-home tapeworm, and a mosquito bite might be all it takes for a parasite that disfigures your testicles to find its way into your bloodstream. Feast your eyes on these ticks, flies, worms, parasites and amoebas that will happily make a meal out of you. Or look away—they're pretty gross.

BRAIN-EATING AMOEBA (NAEGLERIA FOWLERI)

The next time you're in a warm freshwater lake, you might want to skip diving, water skiing or any other activity that could force water up your nose. The nasal passage is the express lane for *N. fowleri*, aka brain-eating amoebas, to travel up your olfactory nerve to your brain's frontal lobe.

To be fair, *these single-celled organisms aren't microscopic zombies looking for brains to eat,* as they usually prefer to eat bacteria found in river and lake sediment. But if presented with no other option, your frontal lobe will do—**the amoeba will begin to multiply as it feeds on your nerve tissue, causing inflammation, death of brain tissue and internal bleeding.** *Without telling you how to live your life, it's an objectively not great way to start your morning.*

Thankfully, **infection is exceedingly rare,** with only 145 cases in the U.S. between 1962 and 2018. But this is unsettling when considered alongside the fact that **the amoeba is extremely common in soil and warm waters** around the world—it grows best in temperatures of up to 115 degrees F—and scientists don't know why only some people become infected.

People have also inadvertently injected their brains with the bacteria by dunking their heads in hot springs or using neti pots filled with untreated water to clear out their nasal passages. The amoeba can also grow in improperly treated pools as well as any tap water that may have become infected and heated.

GIANT KIDNEY WORM (DIOCTOPHYME RENALE)

If their name didn't immediately give it away, giant kidney worms are, in a word, disgusting. **The blood-red roundworms are parasites that can grow up to 40 inches long and will destroy your kidneys and other organs,** if given the chance. Usually these parasites grow to maturity in carnivorous mammals, like minks and dogs, that have eaten a fish or frog carrying the *D. renale* larvae. But on rare occasions, **if a human eats an infected carrier of the larvae, they can also become a host for the parasite**.

According to the CDC, the larvae "migrate" *(a fancy dinner table way of saying "gnaw and wriggle")* through the host's gastric wall to the liver and eventually settle down in the kidneys, where it will take about six months for them to reach adulthood. Mercifully, the chances of this happening to you are much smaller than the parasites themselves, as there have been less than 20 confirmed cases of infection in humans worldwide since the early 1900s.

FUN FACT

In humans, the larvae tend to get sidetracked and settle down in subcutaneous nodules, where they can't develop into adults. On the plus side, this keeps them from destroying your kidneys and potentially killing you. On the creepy side, you'd probably never know they are there.

ASCARIS ROUNDWORM

Ascaris roundworm infections are pretty uncommon in any area with indoor plumbing, **but that doesn't mean you still shouldn't be aware of these tiny worms that want to live in your intestines**, where they can grow big and long—up to 12 inches.

Most infected people don't have any symptoms, though more serious cases of ascaris roundworm infection include **vomiting, nausea, fever, wheezing and coughing**. If you're wondering how you'll be able to tell this is a roundworm infection instead of the stomach flu, take an extra close look at your poop. If you have the parasite, it will be full of tiny roundworm eggs—*and perhaps a worm or 20.*

Though roundworm infections are easily treated, people who don't receive medical attention can wind up with side effects such as volvulus (abnormal twisting of the intestine), intussusception (part of your intestine pulling into itself) and death (you die). But even if you are treated long before these stages, most people prefer not ever having the experience of pooping out foot-long worms. To avoid this fate, don't eat any roundworm eggs—which, as you may recall, have been passed by another infected person. In practice, this means washing your hands, not drinking untreated water, avoiding any raw produce you haven't washed yourself and, obviously, skipping that side order of feces.

WHIPWORM

Though they're best known for infecting our pets, whipworms are also a big problem in humans—**according to the CDC, somewhere around 604 to 795 million people are infected**. Like Ascaris roundworms, this parasite hangs out in your small intestines so you poop out their eggs, potentially passing the infection to someone else. *This, among myriad other reasons, is why you should not use human feces as a fertilizer.*

Technically, whipworm infection is known as **trichuriasis**. Like some other parasites, you may not notice just a few worms. But in serious cases, your body will let you know via frequent, painful passage of stool, mucus, water and blood. Also, rectal prolapse (**your rectum sliding out of your anus and turning inside out**) can occur. We'll say it again—*for the love of all that is holy, wash your hands and wash your produce.*

HOOKWORM

Hookworms are one of the three most common parasites contracted from larvae-poop-contaminated soil. Infections are still common in parts of the world, and until the 1950s, they were particularly prevalent in the southern U.S.

Hookworms wreaked havoc from Texas to West Virginia, where kids often ran around barefoot. The parasite passed more easily in poorer areas, where people were using latrines instead of bedpans. From contaminated soil, the larvae could **burrow directly into a person's feet**, leaving behind sores known as "**ground itch**" or "**dew itch**."

Hookworm infections often create **iron deficiencies**, resulting in exhaustion and an inability to think clearly. As a result it was called "**the germ of laziness**," *a cute nickname that helped stigmatize the South—*and detracted from the realities of parasite-induced anemia increasing the likelihood of death from childbirth or disease.

SCREWWORM

Screwworms, **the parasitic larvae of blowflies,** are one of the nastiest parasites you can be unlucky enough to play host to. **Once a mother fly lays its eggs in an open wound, out hatch the sharp-toothed maggots, ready to slowly eat their host alive.** Then, after the screwworms have worked their way a couple inches deep, they will begin feeding on deeper tissue, like muscles. And the only way to get these tiny flesh-eating maggots out of your body is with tweezers, a process that can take a while—*they don't call them screwworms for no reason.*

Other than open wounds, screwworm eggs can also be laid in any mucus-covered tissue, like your eyes, ears, nostrils or anus. And though human infections are rare (blowflies much prefer to lay their eggs in animals), they do happen.

In one horrifying case that should remind us all to literally cover our asses, a 4-year-old girl in India was treated for an infestation in her rectum, **creating an ulcer about twice the size of a quarter**. Thankfully, doctors removed all the maggots. According to the Department of Pediatrics at RD Gardi Medical College, "[The] wound became maggot-free in four days during which **hundreds of whitish briskly motile maggots measuring 10 to 18 mm** [0.39 to 0.71 inches long] were retrieved."

ACANTHAMOEBA

Some people might think that something **just one cell big** wouldn't be able to do much damage to you. Those people would be very, very wrong, *and probably need to wash their hands a bit more often to keep something like acanthamoeba out of their bodies*. These itty-bitty parasites are found all over the world in just about all water sources, including tap water, lakes, swimming pools and even your heating and air conditioning units, **just waiting to get inside you via a skin ulcer or cut, your nasal passages or even your eyeballs**.

These parasites especially like to wind up in your eyes, resulting in a condition called **Acanthamoeba keratitis**— people who wear contacts are at the highest risk, *especially if they do gross things like rinse their lenses with tap water*. Symptoms include eye pain, redness, blurred vision and sensitivity to light. **If you ignore these signs for long enough, you might go blind**.

The prognosis isn't better if the parasite enters through a wound instead. In rare cases, this can cause granulomatous amebic encephalitis (GAE), a very serious infection in your brain or spinal cord. And though eye and skin infections are usually treatable, GAE is often fatal.

TICKS

The bane of campers everywhere, *ticks can do more than completely disgust you when you find one of their blood-engorged bodies embedded in your skin*—they can also infect you with an array of diseases. No matter which tick-borne illness you have, you're likely to experience **fever, chills, aches and pains**. Many tick-related diseases also come with a rash: Lyme disease, southern tick-associated rash illness, Rocky Mountain spotted fever, ehrlichiosis and tularemia each have distinctive rashes that occur in a majority of cases. **These diseases are all easily treatable, but they are usually difficult for doctors to diagnose**.

These blood-sucking parasites can also cause "**tick paralysis**," which is believed to be caused by **a toxin in tick saliva**. According to the CDC, symptoms include "acute, ascending, flaccid paralysis that is often confused with other neurologic disorders or diseases." Treatment is simple—*you should be able to move normally again within 24 hours of removing the tick.*

TICK TRICKS

The CDC recommends using fine-tipped tweezers to grasp the tick as closely to your skin as possible, then pulling up with steady, even pressure. Don't waste time heating the tweezers or painting the tick with petroleum to make it detach; you want to take it out as quickly as possible.

MANGO FLY

Also known as the tumbu fly or skin maggot fly, **these larvae, common to parts of Africa, will burrow into your skin and begin to feast**. Many people get infected when they put on clothes that have been left out to dry—wet clothes are a favorite place for mango flies to lay their eggs.

Mango flies create **itchiness, insomnia and extreme pain**, plus large sores that look like boils, except for the tiny, pin-sized hole in the center, through which the larvae breathes. Another telltale sign: Sometimes, in the final stages, *you can see the tail of the maggot moving beneath your skin.*

While it's best to remove mango flies ASAP, they will eventually emerge on their own. When the boil bursts, you'll feel the sweet relief of draining pus, blood *and the maggot that caused it all.*

BOTFLY

In case mosquitoes (page 58) hadn't done enough to us, they also occasionally serve as tiny botfly egg carriers—botflies lay their eggs on the bodies of mosquitoes or flies, which then transfer the eggs when biting a person or animal. **Warmed by your skin, the egg immediately hatches**, at which point the tiny larvae dig in for the long haul.

In one disgusting case, a woman returned from her honeymoon in Belize with an unexpected straggler—**a baby botfly growing in her groin**. What she first thought was a pimple became an itchy lesion with a small hole in it. When doctors cut into the lesion, **they extracted a tapered insect with rows of hooks and spines along its body**—a botfly larva. According to Dr. Enrico Camporesi, the woman's doctor, *the hole would have grown much larger if the larva got the chance to emerge as a hairy, half-inch-long adult fly.*

69

TAPEWORMS

Arguably the most famous kind of worm to live in your intestines, **tapeworms can grow to 80 feet in length and survive for up to 30 years in their host**. Usually, humans contract tapeworms by eating raw or undercooked meat from an infected animal. **But there is also another, arguably more disgusting method of contraction:** You can also get them from an infected person who prepared food for you but didn't wash their hands after pooping, *adding an unexpected garnish of tapeworm eggs to your meal.*

If you have an ever-growing worm living inside your body, you may sometimes complain of nausea, weakness, diarrhea, abdominal pain, weight loss and vitamin deficiencies. **But more often, tapeworms don't cause symptoms.** In these cases, the only way you'd know you were infected is if you noticed bits of tapeworms in your own bowel movements. And if you do, tell your doctor immediately—**tapeworm infections are very treatable with medicine that paralyzes the worm,** *making it detach from your intestines so you can evacuate it the next time you go número dos.*

Though further complications from tapeworms infections are rare, **pork tapeworms in particular** can cause some life-threatening destruction to your liver, eyes, heart and brain— *these extra-curious worms sometimes leave your intestines and migrate around to other parts of your body.*

In Victorian England, women occasionally ingested tapeworms to lose weight and then needed to have them removed once their waist was sufficiently tiny. Unfortunately, doctors didn't have a great solution. One doctor invented the method of pushing a cylinder of food down the patient's digestive tract to lure out the worm; as you may have guessed, many woman choked to death from this procedure. Other folk treatments involved trying to lure the tapeworm out from the other end, sometimes by holding a glass of milk to tempt it—this was also probably not very effective. And oh, if you thought no one took tapeworms to lose weight anymore, think again: In 2013, one woman in Iowa perplexed her doctor after admitting she had done just that.

TOXOPLASMOSIS

Like a lot of parasites, **you could have toxoplasmosis and never know it**. As long as you have a healthy immune system, the parasite *Toxoplasma gondii* will have a hard time causing illness—some people will develop flu-like symptoms, but most show no signs of infection. *What the parasite doesn't have a hard time doing, however, is getting around*: More than 40 million people in the U.S. may be infected, according to the CDC.

This parasite is usually picked up by **consuming undercooked, contaminated meat or shellfish, or from changing your cat's litter box**. As it turns out, cats can kill you in a few different ways (page 17), *including with their poop.* Because of this, those with compromised immune systems should be excused from poop-scooping duties—**severe toxoplasmosis can harm your brain, eyes or other organs**. This also goes for pregnant people, as infants born to newly infected women are at risk for being born with serious eye or brain damage.

THE EYES HAVE IT

According to the CDC, even healthy people are at risk for developing eye damage from toxoplasmosis.

FILARIOIDEA

Though these parasites aren't exactly deadly, they do cause **lymphatic filariasis**, a disfiguring disease that affects more than 120 million people in the tropics and subtropics of Asia, Africa, the western Pacific and some areas in South America and the Caribbean. Caused by the *Filarioidea* family of parasitic nematodes, ***these tiny, thread-like worms are usually transferred to humans via public enemy number one: mosquitoes.***

Once they enter your blood, the worms make their way to your lymph nodes to mature. Many people show no symptoms whatsoever, but an unfortunate minority develop **lymphedema, aka fluid collection and swelling in various body parts: usually legs, but sometimes arms, breasts or genitalia**. Those with lymphedema are also more likely to develop bacterial infections, which results in **hardening and thickening of the skin, aka elephantiasis**. Men are also at risk of developing **hydrocele, or swelling of the scrotum**.

It gets worse—though men can undergo surgery to have their balls resized, lymphedema can only be managed. Among advice like disinfecting wounds and washing yourself, the CDC also suggests performing exercises to move the fluid and improve "lymph" flow and wearing shoes that fit your swollen feet.

RAT LUNGWORM

In a disgusting little circle of life, rat lungworms usually mature in the following manner: First, a rat infected with the parasite poops out the larvae; then a snail eats the larvae, allowing it to mature but not become an adult; finally the snail is eaten by another rat, where the parasite can become a fully grown lungworm. **Of course, this circle can go off course if something else eats the snail—like a human**.

Technically called Angiostrongylus cantonensis, this parasitic worm usually makes its way to humans when someone accidentally swallows a tiny snail in raw produce, eats some undercooked escargot or swallows an infected snail during a game of "Truth or Dare." You should probably always refuse a dare to eat a wild snail, but *definitely* choose truth if you're in Asia, the Pacific Islands, the Caribbean or Africa, where cases of infection have been recorded.

Usually, rat lungworm dies of its own accord—according to the CDC, most cases don't require treatment. But in rare cases, the infection can cause *eosinophilic meningitis*. An Australian man ate a snail on a dare and contracted this **rare form of meningitis**. The man was comatose for more than a year, developed a severe brain infection and became paralyzed from the neck down before dying.

LIVER FLUKE

If you're ever abroad, *you may want to stick with the Land Lover's section of the menu.* Eating raw or undercooked fish, crabs or crayfish from certain areas could result in ingesting a liver fluke, **a parasite that wants to find its new home in your liver**. But first it will have to travel from your intestine and **burrow its way through your liver's lining**. And yes, you'll feel this via some pain in your upper right abdomen.

Other symptoms of a fluke living it up in your organs include **nausea, vomiting, diarrhea, hives and malaise**. These freeloaders can also clog up your bile ducts and lay eggs, causing abdominal pain that might last as long as 30 years. *If all of this sounds like something you'd rather avoid*, you should also be wary of eating freshwater fish and drinking or washing your produce with contaminated water.

GUINEA WORM

Though Guinea worm disease, aka *dracunculiasis*, is rarely fatal in humans, it can make you sick for months—*in fact, you may get a little sick just reading about it*. Now a relatively rare disease on its way to eradication, guinea worm disease still occurs in Chad, Ethiopia, Mali and South Sudan.

This parasite spreads when people drink **water contaminated with Guinea worm larvae**, *which hang out in your body until they're ready to emerge about a year later*. Swelling, blistering and ulcers form at the eruption site, which is usually on your leg or foot. As a bonus, **this can be extra-debilitating if the ulcer becomes infected**, or lead to permanent disability if the worm decides to exit via one of your joints.

The worm comes out very slowly—according to the CDC, **it can be pulled out just a few centimeters each day**. Getting the whole worm out can take as little as a few days, *but usually takes weeks*.

SCHISTOSOME

Schistosomes, *aka tiny worms that want to live in your blood vessels and lay eggs all over your body*, are found in sources of freshwater all over the world. This includes Brazil, Suriname, Venezuela, parts of the Caribbean, parts of the Middle East, southern China, parts of southeast Asia and the Philippines, and southern and sub-Saharan Africa. If that sounds like a lot of places, that's because it is—according to the CDC, **more than 200 million people are currently infected**.

Water becomes contaminated with these parasites when an infected person pees or poops in the water, leading to the depositing of tiny eggs. If a certain kind of snail lives in the water, the parasites can mature into worms. *Then it's game over for anyone who even wades in the water*—schistosomes can penetrate right through your skin, giving you **schistosomiasis**.

Those with schistosomiasis usually show no signs early on, though you could experience a rash or flu-like symptoms. The real problems begin when the parasites travel to your intestine, liver, lungs or bladder, which can cause severe damage if untreated. If you're unlucky enough to have a schistosome laying eggs in your brain or spinal cord, you could experience seizures, inflammation of your spinal cord or even paralysis.

LEISHMANIA

Leishmania parasites are usually carried by **sand flies**, *which unfortunately, are basically the ninjas of the fly world.* Not only are they exceptionally small—**about a quarter of the size of the average mosquito or sometimes smaller**—they are also silent and can have painless bites. In other words, they can infect you with **leishmaniasis** and you might not have any idea for weeks, months or even years, when symptoms begin to develop.

Leishmaniasis can take two forms. In **cutaneous leishmaniasis**, infected people develop sores that "can change in size and appearance over time," according to the CDC. **Sores may start out as bumps or lumps and end up as ulcers.** They eventually heal on their own, but that can take months or years and may leave "ugly scars." Some types of the parasite can also cause sores in the mucous membranes of your mouth, nose or throat. **It's pretty unpleasant and usually painful**, *but at least it's not deadly.*

On the other hand, this parasite can also result in **visceral leishmaniasis**, which usually affects your liver (*bad*), spleen (*also bad*) and bone marrow (*all kinds of bad*). It can result in weight loss, fever, swelling of the liver and spleen and low blood counts. **If untreated, this form of the disease is often fatal.**

GNATHOSTOMA

People most commonly become hosts to gnathostoma parasites when they eat raw or undercooked meat from an infected animal, **usually fish**. If you become a host for these worms, the first potential signs will be the stomach pain, nausea, vomiting or diarrhea that occur—*all of these are results of the worms burrowing through your stomach or intestine to your liver*.

Next, the worm larvae, which can't fully mature in your body, will settle under your skin, **resulting in red, painful and itchy swellings**. This stage can occur as soon as 3 to 4 weeks after infection, but if your worms choose to procrastinate, *it may not occur for as many as 10 years*.

If you're wildly unfortunate, these worms will enter other parts of your body, like your lungs, bladder, ears, eyes or brain. Depending on where they wander, you could go blind, become parlyzed, fall into a coma or die.

FILET-O-SICK

If you're in Asia, skip the ceviche—marinating infected fish in lime juice won't kill any parasites. However, the CDC says sushi, which is usually made from saltwater fish, is probably fine. Probably.

TOXOCARA

If your dog or cat has **Toxocara worms**, they're not the only ones at risk. These parasites like to hang out in the intestines of your furry companions, who then poop out the eggs. Then you (*or more likely, any young kids you may have*) become infected when they eat dirt contaminated with the cat or dog poop. Rarely, people can also become hosts for the parasite by **eating undercooked, infected meat**.

Most infected people show no symptoms whatsoever. But those who do get sick either develop **visceral toxocariasis** (*the larvae take a trip to some of your organs*, resulting in fever, coughing, wheezing, abdominal pain and fatigue) or **ocular toxocariasis** (*the larvae visit your eyes*, causing vision loss, eye inflammation or damage to the retina). According to a CDC report from 2011, **about 70 people in the U.S. are blinded by this parasite each year**.

RHINOSPORIDIUM SEEBERI

If you've been swimming in freshwaters in southern India, Sri Lanka or southeast Asia and now have a **slow-growing polyp** (*aka fleshy mass*) coming out of your nose or eye, *congratulations!*—there's a good chance you've been infected with **R. seeberi**, a type of aquatic parasite. Polyps caused by **R. seeberi** are usually deep red or pink in color and tend to bleed easily.

This scenario is the most common way **R. seeberi** is contracted and presented, but cases have also been reported in South America, the U.S. and Africa. You can also develop **wart-like lesions on your skin, ears, genitals or rectum**, and, in rare cases, according to Stanford University, "*profuse dissemination occurs throughout the body, which can be life threatening.*"

> ### THEY'LL BE BACK
> Rhinosporidiosis is treated by surgically removing the polyps, but relapse occurs in about 10 percent of cases.

SPIROMETRA ERINACEIEUROPAEI

Technically a kind of tapeworm, this parasite rarely makes it into humans—**just 300 cases have been reported since 1953**. They're so rare because humans don't easily fit into their life cycle, which involves infecting crustaceans, which get eaten by reptiles and amphibians, which then get eaten by cats, dogs and other carnivores. And though they're usually found in China, Japan, South Korea and Thailand, scientists generally believe these tapeworms are **cosmopolitan**, meaning they have a worldwide distribution. *No word as of yet on whether they also go to swanky rooftop parties.*

When this parasite does wind up in humans, they don't spend their time in the gut like they usually would in other animals. **Instead, they may migrate just about anywhere:** under your skin, in your lungs or even in breast lumps— apparently, some women have gone to the doctor with breast cancer fears, *only to be relieved and horrified to find out they've got a tapeworm copping a feel.*

Spirometra erinaceieuropaei will also occasionally make their way to a person's brain, where they live off the tissue's fatty acids. *If it's any consolation, these tapeworms aren't exactly eating your brain or any other part of your body*—instead, they absorb nutrients directly through their skin.

Around 2010, a Chinese man was admitted to a U.K. hospital for seizures, headaches, an altered sense of smell and memory flashbacks. Doctors had a hard time diagnosing him—MRIs showed an "abnormal region" but no tumor—and the man lived with these symptoms over the next four years, until later MRIs showed the region was moving. Around. In. His. Brain. According to *New Scientist*, after the doctors finally decided to operate, "they pulled out a 1-centimeter-long ribbon-shaped worm." If you ever contract one of these parasites, you'll likely need surgery too—according to genome sequencing, they're resistant to benzimidazole, the conventional drug used for tapeworm treatment.

SCABIES

Also known as the **human itch mite**, *scabies aren't an infection as much as an infestation*. The microscopic mites **burrow into the upper layer of your skin and then lay eggs**, resulting in an intensely itchy, pimple-like rash that can also include tiny blisters and scales. Scabies can make their way into your skin anywhere, but common places include the **wrist, armpit, fingers, webbing between your fingers, nipples, penis, waist and butt**.

If you have scabies for the first time, you may not show symptoms for 4 to 6 weeks, *but you are still capable of spreading the bug love*. Scabies are shared via direct skin contact and **thrive in crowded conditions**, making outbreaks fairly common in nursing homes, extended-care facilities, prisons and childcare facilities.

If you contract scabies and have a weak immune system, you may end up with a more severe infestation known as "crusted scabies," which is as bad as it sounds: a thick crust of skin filled with a large amount of scabies mites and eggs.

CLOSE CONTACT

Usually, it takes prolonged skin contact to transmit scabies from one person to another, but if you so much as shake hands with someone who has crusted scabies, you should see a doctor.

LICE

If you have sores on your head, feel something moving around in your hair and have been spending time with kindergartners, there's a good chance you have lice. **Whether they're crawling around on your head or your genitals,** lice infestations are annoying, itchy and shudder-inducing, but not exactly deadly. (*Then again, the knowledge you may have been hosting a colony of bugs on your head for 4 to 6 weeks before anything even itched might make you a little crazy.*)

Less common but more concerning are **body lice**. Body lice, *which are unlikely to hang out on anyone who has regular access to a shower and clean clothes*, can cause thickened and discolored skin in heavily bitten areas of your body and sores that can easily become infected. And while head lice and pubic lice can't spread disease, body lice can: **epidemic typhus, trench fever and louse-borne relapsing fever** are their calling cards.

CRAB WALK OF SHAME

According to Planned Parenthood, millions of people are infected with pubic lice, or "crabs," every year. The itchy-but-harmless lice can also live in your eyelashes, eyebrows, armpits, chest hair, mustache or beard. Thankfully, recent body grooming trends have led to a general reduction in the crab population.

TRICHOMONAS VAGINALIS

The pesky protozoan parasite that causes **trichomoniasis**, aka "trich," is very common but also very treatable—*if you bother to treat it*. Only about 30 percent of people who have trich develop symptoms, and **about 3.7 million people in the U.S. have the disease.**

Like a lot of other STDs, trich symptoms are, in a word, nasty. Men can expect irritation or itching inside the penis, a burning sensation after ejaculation or urination and "discharge from the penis," according to the CDC. Women's symptoms are similar: genital burning, itching, soreness and redness; painful urination; and unusual vaginal discharge, including discharge that is yellow or green with a fishy smell.

More concerningly, **pregnant women who have trich are more likely to give birth too early or to have underweight babies**. Trich also makes it easier to pass on or contract **HIV** (page 162). On the plus side, trich is very easily treated—just make sure your partner is treated as well, *or else you risk reinfection.*

IT'S TRICH-Y

Though wearing a condom reduces the risk of passing on trich, you're far from fully protected— these parasites can still infect areas not covered by a condom.

ENTEROBIASIS PINWORM

Also known as a **threadworm**, this type of roundworm is fond of living inside people's rectums or colons—*you know, where it's nice and warm*. While the infected person is sleeping, **female pinworms leave the intestine to lay their eggs on the skin just outside the butthole**, causing itching and a generally restless night. This is ideal for the pinworm—the fingers you used to scratch yourself are now covered in **pinworm egg**s, ready to infect other people.

You don't even need to directly touch someone with your unwashed fingers to spread the eggs—according to the CDC, pinworm eggs are so small **they can become airborne**, causing others to ingest them while breathing. Unsurprisingly, **pinworm is the most common worm infection in the U.S.**, with children under 18, people who take care of those children and those who are institutionalized making up the majority of cases.

If you're wondering whether your itchy butt is caused by pinworms, **try the CDC's "tape test."** As soon as you wake up, firmly press clear tape to the skin around your anus. (*Seriously—you can't make this stuff up.*) Any eggs will stick to the tape, which you can then take to your doctor to get inspected under a microscope. **Check three mornings in a row for best results.**

BED BUGS

The apartment-ruiningest creatures since plague-carrying mice, **bed bugs reduce entire cities to fear and paranoia with the mere mention of their name**. The insanely prolific creatures—*whose only nourishment is, charmingly, blood*—were once thought to be a problem confined to developing nations. But according to the CDC, outbreaks in the U.S., Canada and all over Europe have proven bed bugs don't really care where you come from. *They want to crawl into bed with you because of who you are on the inside*: a skin sack full of delicious AB negative.

While it's unlikely bed bugs will lead to your demise, some allergic reactions can cause nasty side effects like infection and anaphylaxis. But death isn't the bed bug's aim. Instead, they effectively, if unintentionally, *engage in pure psychological warfare*. "Bed bugs are experts at hiding," says the CDC. "Their slim flat bodies allow them to fit into the smallest of spaces and stay there for long periods of time, even without a blood meal." What's more, bed bugs are so small their bites often don't show up on the skin of those who have been bitten. **So how can you tell if you're infested?**

The easiest ways to spot the creatures are by their shed exoskeletons or, best of all, **by the rusty-colored, blood-based Number Twos** they leave on your sheets or the edges of your mattress as they burrow back to their hidey holes. Bed bugs can travel up to 100 feet at night when they're active, **but tend to make their homes within 8 feet of where a human sleeps**. *Cozy*. If you think you've noticed signs of bed buggery around your sleeping area, contact an experienced exterminator and check pretty much everything in your bedroom for bugs. *Oh, and try to avoid the temptation to burn everything you own.*

BOUGIE BLOODSUCKERS

When guests check into the five-star accommodations at New York hotels like the Waldorf Astoria or the Marriott Marquis, they expect an experience they'll never forget in the Big Apple. And in 2016, according to the British tabloid *The Daily Mail*, more than 40 guests at these hotels and more of the highest-priced hotels in the city got exactly that. They probably didn't expect to turn down the sheets and find their 1,600 thread count Egyptian cotton sheets crawling with bed bugs. How's that for memorable? In the Marriott's defense, bed bugs are notoriously difficult to exterminate, and the task isn't getting easier—Louis Sorkin, an entomologist at the American Museum of Natural History, says the little buggers "have increasingly become resistant to insecticides."

NATURAL DISASTERS

Living things aren't the only tools in Mother Nature's torture kit. She could boil you in ash and lava, roast you in a wildfire, crush you under the weight of a meteorite, freeze you to death in a blizzard or cause everything you own to crush you during a massive earthquake. The worst part? That's all stuff that could happen while you're sitting on your couch.

QUICKSAND

In one of nature's fun twists on logic, quicksand is **sand that has become so saturated with water that it essentially acts as a liquid.** And since you can't stand on a pile of liquid without sinking, you can't stand on quicksand without sinking either—at least, to a point.

Unlike what you've seen in the movies, quicksand would never actually pull you all the way under. You can thank the rules of density and physics for that—**quicksand has a density of about 2 grams per milliliter, while humans are less dense at 1 gram per milliliter.** In layman's terms, this means you'll sink up to your waist, but going any farther is like trying to shove a beach ball underwater.

That being said, quicksand is still an excellent trap. And again, unlike the movies, just having your friends toss you a rope (*or a large snake, Dr. Jones*) and pull you out is a bad idea. Daniel Bonn, a physics professor at the Van der Waals-Zeeman Institute at the University of Amsterdam who coauthored a study on quicksand, says **rescuers would probably pull you "into two pieces" if they were to just yank you out.** Bonn instead suggests slowly and continually wiggling your legs around to create a space for water to flow, loosening the sand and allowing you to wriggle free. And if you're trapped in quicksand near the ocean, where it's more likely to form, you better get moving—death by drowning from the incoming tide is a real possibility.

In February 2019, 34-year-old Ryan Osmun was hiking with his friend Jessika McNeill in Utah's Zion National Park. Hiking in winter conditions is already dangerous, but it's even worse when someone steps in quicksand— Osmun sank up to his knee. When McNeill was unable to help him out, she had to hike for three more hours before finally getting cell service to call 911. By then it had already started to snow. It took a few more hours for the rescue crew to locate Osmun, then at least two hours to free him. After being treated for exposure, hypothermia and extremity injuries, Osmun later told reporters that being trapped was like "standing in a huge puddle of concrete that basically just dries instantly.... There was no chance of moving it at all."

HURRICANES

According to National Hurricane Center meteorologist Joel Cline, *the best way to survive a hurricane is to get out of its way.* As Cline explains it, heeding an evacuation warning is your best bet—**once the storm surge arrives, your odds of survival get a whole lot worse.** This was part of the problem in the **Great Galveston Storm of 1900**, the worst natural disaster in American history. No one had any idea how bad the storm would be, leading to the deaths of somewhere between 6,000 and 12,000 people.

EXTRA ELEMENTS

Hurricanes also come with vast amounts of rain, contributing to flooding, plus strong winds that are capable of killing you—usually via flying debris.

Storm surges are the vast amounts of water that get pushed on shore during a hurricane. And being able to swim won't necessarily save you from the severe flooding that comes with them—**water weighs about 1,700 pounds per cubic yard,** making a severe hurricane's 20-foot waves more than capable of decimating buildings that haven't been designed to take that kind of beating. *And, if you haven't tried, it's tough to outswim a falling building.*

TORNADOES

If humid, warm air crashes into dry, cold air—something that happens quite often when large thunderstorms come in contact with the warm ground—you could have a tornado on your hands. These terrifying towers of violent wind are notoriously hard to predict, with an **average warning time of just 13 minutes.**

This is far from enough time to evacuate an area, **but enough time to take cover in an underground shelter**. And if you're dealing with a twister that's 660 feet wide with 300-miles-per-hour winds, *underground is the best place to be.*

These powerful, car-tossing winds often end in a few seconds, but some tornadoes go on for hours. *And while you could be whipped around before being dropped from a dangerous height*, **you'd probably be killed by flying debris.**

EARTHQUAKE

If you ever feel like you're on shaky ground, *it might be because you literally are*. Earth's surface is anything but stable—**it's made up of tectonic plates that are constantly bumping into one another**, causing earthquakes (and volcanoes [page 98], landslides [page 100] and more). In fact, thousands of quakes that are too small to be noticed happen every day.

Mother Nature tosses us a bone by only bringing on the giant ones every 5 to 10 years, but lesser quakes—which can still collapse buildings and cause all kinds of wreckage—**claim the lives of about 10,000 people each year.**

NOW LEAN BACK

People can't predict earthquakes, but they can prepare for them. Engineers are trying to minimize damage by constructing buildings designed to sway under the stress of earthquakes.

AVALANCHE

As anyone who has ever made a snowball knows, not all snow is created equal. Some is powdery and difficult to pack together; **some clumps together into snowballs that can crack your skull**. And as Brian Lazar, deputy director at the Colorado Avalanche Information Center, explains, **the wrong combination of these kinds of snow on the side of a mountain can be problematic**: "When you're loading weak layers at the bottom of the snowpack with heavy snow on top, that's conducive for creating avalanches. **When you build any kind of structure, you don't want to have a weak foundation**, and with snowpack, it's really no different."

JUST A SLUFF

A mini avalanche, aka a "sluff," happens when loose, powdery snow tumbles down the side of a mountain. Sluffs don't usually cause much damage to property or people.

Avalanches happen all the time as snow melts or heavier snow just becomes too much for the weaker layers below to support, but **most fatal avalanches occur when people trigger them by snowboarding, skiing or snowmobiling** on a cold, slippery death trap. *If you're the kind of person who thinks it's fun to strap some wood to your feet and throw yourself down a mountain, make sure you're doing it with friends.* Hopefully at least one of you doesn't get buried and can dig everyone else out—**you'll have about 18 minutes to live before dying of asphyxiation from breathing in your own exhaled air.**

BLIZZARD

Multiple feet of snow, temps of –50 degrees F and winds at 70 miles per hour can kill you in a whole lot of ways. The most obvious is **freezing to death**—according to Dr. Robert Glatter, an emergency physician at Lenox Hill Hospital in New York City, a healthy person who isn't properly dressed for cold weather could become **hypothermic** in as little as 10 minutes when temperatures drop to -30 degrees F.

Mild hypothermia begins when your body temperature drops to 95 degrees F. As you get colder and your **heart, brain and other organs stop working properly**, you can also experience amnesia, lose consciousness *and eventually turn into a human Popsicle like Jack Torrance in* The Shining.

Other ways to die include having a **heart attack** when shoveling snow, **freezing or suffocating in your car** after you've pulled over because of bad roads or **cracking your head open** after slipping and falling on ice.

ICICLE

Even though they're very pretty, *you should never admire icicles from below.* You've probably walked under icicles and survived unscathed, but you never know when one might break off, **sending its icy point right through your body**. Death by icicle isn't exactly common, but it does happen, *and not just in* Die Hard 2.

In 2012, a woman in Belgrade died after being impaled by a **nine-pound icicle**. In 2010, there were **five icicle-related deaths** and more than 150 injuries in Saint Petersburg, Russia. In the U.S., Chicago seems to have the most icicle injuries—harsh winters and tall buildings mean **ice daggers can fall for more than 1,000 feet before they hit you.**

According to the *Chicago Tribune*, this exact scenario happened in 1994 when a chunk of ice *"the size of a microwave"* fell off the Neiman Marcus on Michigan Avenue, **hitting a man in the head and killing him immediately**.

DROUGHT

Despite what you may have heard, plants don't crave electrolytes—plants, and pretty much everything else that's alive, crave water. **And if they don't get enough of it, they die.** Lack of rainwater means less to drink and nothing to water crops and livestock with, which in turn creates a lack of food. That's a bad situation—*as you probably know, people require both food and water to live.*

Droughts can also increase the spread of **communicable diseases**—without fresh water, sanitation standards drop dramatically. According to WHO, this means an increase in the spread of **cholera** (page 152), **typhoid fever, acute respiratory infections and measles**.

Unfortunately, people have a hard time preparing for droughts when their economy is entirely dependent on **agriculture.** According to the World Meteorological Organization, **droughts killed almost 680,000 people between 1970 and 2012.**

HEAT WAVE

Much like Goldilocks and her porridge, the human body doesn't like to be too hot or too cold—we like 98.6 degrees F, **aka "just right."** If your body exceeds 104 degrees F, you'll probably have **heatstroke**. Signs include vomiting, confusion, slurred speech, seizures and even going comatose. Without treatment, you'll do damage to your vital organs and die.

While it's not surprising you can get heatstroke by just existing in **skin-melting temperatures**—especially if you're somewhere like **California's Death Valley,** which has a record high of 134—*people can also get heatstroke in much less crazy conditions*. In May 2019, at least five people died in Japan (and nearly 600 were hospitalized) when the heat reached just 103.

Even more moderate temperatures can be deadly if people don't take proper precautions—**exercising and lack of hydration in hot weather both increase the likelihood of heatstroke.**

WILDFIRE

Wildfires can occur naturally—**a bolt of lightning in a dried-out forest can spark the deadly flames,** and they're especially common in areas like the western U.S., where drought, heat and thunderstorms are all regular occurrences—*but Smokey Bear wasn't kidding when he said people shoulder the blame for 9 out of 10 forest fires.* Lightning is Mother Nature's choice for starting a blaze, but **arson, campfires, a tossed cigarette or even a downed power line** will do just as well.

OH, BOISE

Though California wildfires are all the rage these days, a 1996 wildfire blazed for a full seven days in the foothills around Boise, Idaho. About 15,000 acres of land and two major watersheds were lost in the fires.

Once a wildfire gets going, high winds and endless fuel make it incredibly difficult to extinguish. This is especially true in areas like Northern California, which boasts the deadly combination of steep, tree-covered mountains, brush-covered hillsides and long periods of drought. *Wildfire also moves a lot faster than you probably can*—up to 14 miles per hour—and, according to *National Geographic*, has burned up to 9 million acres of land in recent years.

VOLCANO

There are about 1,500 active volcanoes scattered around the Earth, and 161 within the U.S. Some are much less deadly than others—Hawaii's Kilauea volcano, for example, had an **"effusive eruption"** in 2018. This meant it poured out a steady stream of lava, essentially creating **rivers of magma** that are fairly easy to outrun. **Explosive eruptions**, on the other hand, are the type that leveled Pompeii in 79 A.D.

In an explosive eruption, gasses are trapped in molten rock, **building pressure until the volcano explodes and sends an avalanche of ash, toxic gas and hot rocks hurtling down at speeds up to 450 miles per hour**. Volcanic eruptions can also birth mudflows called **lahars**. *According to National Geographic, the amount of mud and debris from these mudflows can bury an entire town.*

If you manage to escape the rivers of lava and mud, you still have **volcanic ash** to contend with. Unlike wood ash, volcanic ash is not soft. It's made up of tiny pointy fragments of rocks and volcanic glass. Not only is it **dangerous to inhale**, it builds up quickly and is surprisingly heavy— volcanic ash is a pain to shovel away, can cause power outages and **has even caused weak buildings to collapse**.

FROM THE ASHES

Death by lava may be one of the more horrifying ways to go, but we should also be grateful for the periodic eruptions: Volcanoes created more than 80 percent of the Earth's surface, and when volcanic rock breaks down, it makes for incredibly fertile soil.

Mount Vesuvius gets all the attention, but the deadliest eruption in history occurred in 1815 in Indonesia. The explosion of Mount Tabora created a caldera, or crater, 4 miles in diameter and more than 3,600 feet deep. It also blasted hot gas and ash 28 miles high, creating multiple "pyroclastic flows," aka rivers of molten rocks, ash and toxic gas. About 10,000 people died immediately, but approximately 82,000 more died thanks to the eruption's effects: So much ash and gas was in the atmosphere that it literally obscured the sun, cooling the Earth's surface and causing "the year without a summer," a time in which starvation and disease were rampant.

LANDSLIDE

Much like avalanches (page 94), landslides occur when a lot of heavy stuff, like **rocks, soil and other debris**, is on a slope and supported by a weak layer. Landslides are triggered by things like **volcanic activity, earthquakes, heavy rainfall** *or Stevie Nicks climbing a mountain and then turning around.*

Both landslides and their messier cousins, mudslides, are more likely to occur on **slopes that lack vegetation,** usually as a result of wildfire or humans clearing the land. Buildings in such areas are particularly vulnerable. In 2019 in La Paz, Bolivia, **dozens of brick homes built into a hillside were swept away by a particularly large landslide**. Luckily, the neighborhood had evacuated before the incident—experts expected a landslide after the area experienced heavy rains.

T.G.I. MUDSLIDES

While the cocktail version of a mudslide is usually made with chocolate, coffee and rum, actual mudslides occur when heavy rains saturate the ground, making the upper layer much heavier than the supporting layer beneath it. Both can theoretically kill you; only one will make you vomit.

CLIFF

In case you needed another reason to be mad at gravity, the Earth is full of cliffs just waiting for you to slip and fall from. And of course, people can't be content to look at cliffs from below—we insist on standing at their edge, **putting our lives at the mercy of an errant shoelace**.

Distressingly, **some people take the risk beyond just standing there**. Out of the 55 people who had fallen off the Grand Canyon as of 2015, eight were **jumping from one rock to another** or posing for pictures. One man even **pretended to fall** to scare his daughter, before actually tumbling 400 feet to his death.

To decrease your risk of falling off a cliff, don't climb over any guard rails, don't turn around to take a selfie, and generally give yourself enough space to not slip and fall to your death in case you trip over your own feet.

TSUNAMI

Caused by earthquakes, underwater landslides, volcanic eruptions or even meteorites falling in the ocean, tsunamis are **terrifyingly tall waves that are capable of incredible destruction**. They can reach more than 100 feet, *making it seem like a nine-story liquid building is about to crash down around you.*

Tsunamis are most common in and around the Pacific Ocean's "**Ring of Fire**," an area where tectonic shifts regularly cause earthquakes and volcanic eruptions. Once formed, **a tsunami will travel 500 miles per hour**, meaning they can cross the Pacific in less than a day. And thanks to their short wavelength, **they'll lose very little energy as they travel closer to civilization**.

One of the best **warning signs** is the sudden retreating of sea water near the coast—this means the low point of the tsunami has just arrived, *and the rest of the giant wave is only five minutes away.*

LIGHTNING

Getting struck by lightning is very rare and definitely deadly, *but perhaps not as fatal as you think*. According to the National Weather Service, **only 10 percent of people struck by lightning are killed**, though surviving does likely mean living with a disability. Side effects of being hit by lightning include **crazy scars from burst blood vessels**, third-degree burns, **temporary or permanent paralysis**, ruptured eardrums, **personality changes**, mood swings, memory loss, chronic pain and muscle twitches.

And oh, it's also incredibly painful. According to one survivor, it feels like "the pain of a thousand wasps stinging from within." On top of all this, you may be embarrassed to be found partially naked—the air around you will have been superheated to an unbelievable 50,000 degrees F, leaving your clothes in tatters.

Of course, you may not get the chance to experience any of these side effects if you're part of the 10 percent who die upon being hit by lightning. Cardiac arrest is a common cause of death, **though there is also a very real chance of your brain being cooked if the electric current enters your skull**.

SO METAL

If you're wearing any metal when you get struck by lightning, it will probably become superheated and burn your skin. All the more reason to keep rocking that friendship bracelet you made at summer camp.

METEORITE

Shockingly, there are **no verified reports** of a person ever having died from being hit by a meteorite. (*There's a first time for everything, though.*) Still, these rocks from space could definitely kill you if you managed to be standing in the wrong place at the wrong time—they slow down quite a bit by the time they reach Earth but can **still travel at 200 to 400 miles per hour** before they collide with something.

While even a small meteorite could be fatal if it hits you directly, *it's the large ones that have inadvertently led to a lot of deaths.* A giant meteorite falling into the ocean can cause a **tsunami** (page 101), which is capable of killing thousands. And in February 2013, **a massive meteorite/small asteroid exploded over Chelyabinsk, Russia**. The meteorite disintegrated as it entered Earth's atmosphere, **causing a blast stronger than a nuclear explosion**, shattering glass in cars and windows and injuring about 1,200 people.

In 1954, a woman named Ann Hodges survived being hit by a small meteorite while napping in her living room in Alabama. The space rock broke through her ceiling, bounced off a radio and hit her left hip.

RADON

Like something out of a dystopian novel, **radon is a colorless, odorless and tasteless gas that gives you lung cancer, and it's just about everywhere.** It is naturally occurring—radon is produced as uranium found in rocks and soil breaks down— but **just like the carbon dioxide you're constantly breathing out**, it's only dangerous in large quantities.

Unfortunately, **radon is found in large quantities in a lot of places.** According to the U.S. Environmental Protection Agency, nearly 1 in every 15 homes has radon levels that exceed 4 pCi/L, which is the maximum level recommended by the EPA. *While four sounds like a low number, it's actually pretty high*—according to radon testing company Air Chek, Inc., "A family whose home has radon levels of 4 pCi/L is exposed to **approximately 35 times as much radiation as the Nuclear Regulatory Commission would allow if that family was standing next to the fence of a radioactive waste site**."

The only way to find out if you're being exposed to high levels of radon is by testing your home, workplace and anywhere else you spend large quantities of time. Or you could wait to see if you get lung cancer—radon is the second leading cause of the disease, after smoking cigarettes.

LIMNIC ERUPTION

If you've never heard of a limnic eruption, it's probably because they're incredibly rare. As far as scientists know, they can only happen in three places, and there are only two recorded cases in recent history. Both took place in Cameroon in the 1980s, *when lakes essentially burped up giant clouds of toxic gas.* The first explosion at **Lake Monoun** killed just 37 people, but the second explosion at **Lake Nyos** was much more deadly.

Limnic eruptions only occur when a lake absorbs massive amounts of carbon dioxide. Lake Nyos, **which developed in the crater of an inactive volcano**, got its CO_2 from the volcano's occasional leaks. *Like a bottle of Diet Coke someone dropped a Mentos into,* something eventually triggered the lake's eruption and released somewhere between 1 and 3 million tons of CO_2 into the air. **Then the CO_2, which is heavier than regular air, rolled down the mountains and into the nearby village, suffocating about 1,700 people and 3,500 livestock.**

DOOR TO HELL

Also known as the **Darvaza gas crater**, this pit in Turkmenistan is literally **a 230-foot-wide crater that has been continuously burning since 1971**. Geologists were drilling for natural gas when the ground underneath their rig gave way, **opening a crater full of methane**. To keep the flammable gas from entering our atmosphere and suffocating the nearby wildlife, *the scientists lit it on fire.* Clearly, there was much more gas than they expected, **as the inferno has been going for more than 45 years and there's no end in sight**.

The Door to Hell has since become a **tourist attraction**—according to the *Smithsonian*, hundreds of people make the trek each year. The pit doesn't seem to have killed any people, *though it's a little hard to believe no one has ever dumped a body in a fiery hell pit in the middle of a desert.*

RIP CURRENT

Rip currents are commonly mislabeled as **riptides**, *but knowing what to call them won't do you much good when you're being steadily dragged out to sea.* Though they're much subtler than hurricanes or typhoons, rip currents can be as deadly as any storm, and even more so in some areas—according to a 2013 study, **these silent but deadly waters have killed more Australians each year than bushfires, floods, cyclones and shark attacks combined.**

Rip currents are notoriously difficult to spot, leading to thousands of people requiring rescue from them at U.S. beaches each year. However, most of these rescues are only necessary because people panic and attempt to swim directly against the current, which is impossible— *even Olympic swimmers would be pushed back by a current that strong.* In these cases, people quickly exhaust themselves and eventually drown.

BEWARE THE WAVE

Rip currents form for lots of reasons, but a common factor is waves. If there are no breaking waves, you're in a rip current–free zone.

Historically, people have been advised to **swim parallel to the shore** until they have broken free from the current, at which point they can swim back normally. However, **expert Jamie MacMahan suggests just relaxing**, if you can—80 to 90 percent of rip currents run in a circular motion, meaning they'll carry you right back to shore in a few minutes. *Of course, there's still a small chance this won't happen and you'll be hundreds of yards away from shore when the current finally subsides.*

BOG

Bogs are a little like **quicksand**—they look like solid ground, but they're actually more like floating carpets of soil, full of decomposing plant matter and water. In fact, **extra water-logged bogs can be 90 percent water**, meaning hikers might step into what looks like a puddle and wind up stuck up to their waists in decaying plants and stagnant water—*not exactly where you want to be.*

The first step to getting out of a bog? Don't panic. Your flailing will only serve to exhaust you and drag you deeper. If it helps, remember that drowning is unlikely—**most bog-related deaths are caused by exhaustion and hypothermia**.

The key to getting yourself out is **slow, steady movements**. Free your legs one at a time, even if you're only moving inch by inch. If you manage to get out of the bog, resist the urge to walk—**crawl away** until you're sure you're back on solid ground.

DEEP WATER

As the great poet Ludacris once asked, "How low can you go?" The answer, according to science, is usually **about 400 feet below sea level**, though not for very long. While you can survive at those depths (with scuba gear, of course), the pressure is still wreaking havoc on your body—**for every 33 feet you descend, the pressure increases by 14.5 pounds per square inch**. And while deep sea creatures are made for that kind of pressure, humans are not. By about 100 feet, your lung tissue begins to contract, triggering a "**dive response**" where your body sends more blood to your chest to balance the pressure. If you go too low, **your lungs simply collapse**.

There's also the risk of developing **nitrogen narcosis**, a condition in which breathing certain gases at high pressure causes you *to act like you just dropped acid*. In 2000, a Russian diver died after nitrogen narcosis led him to panic and **remove his breathing apparatus at 300 feet below sea level**.

RIVER

While you can drown just about anywhere there's water, rivers are the most common place to breathe in too much hydrogen with your oxygen. In Australia, **858 people drowned in rivers, creeks and streams between 2005 and 2015**, with the second-highest number of fatalities (516) occurring at beaches.

Most deaths occur because people don't take the proper precautions **or fail to realize how deep a river or creek is**. Depths aren't the only problem—according to one expert, **many drownings occur when someone dives into a creek and hits the bottom**. At least one study partially blames alcohol. Between 2002 and 2012, 41 percent of river-drowning victims had been drinking before they went in the water. *(Don't drink and dive, people.)*

Of course, rivers aren't deadly only in Australia. In Buffalo, New York, **people regularly drown after they ignore posted warning signs and hop into the Niagara River**. According to *The Buffalo News*, the river's currents can reach 12 miles per hour, though they appear to look very calm.

FRIGHT WATER RAFTING

Though white water rafting is (somewhat) safe with experienced guides, lax regulations in places like Costa Rica can make it much more dangerous. In 2018, 14 men traveled to Costa Rica for a bachelor party that included white water rafting down the Naranjo River. Things quickly went awry when all three of their boats capsized almost immediately—the river was elevated due to heavy rainfall. Tragically, four of the friends and one guide did not survive.

FLOOD

Floods happen when a lot of water inundates land that's usually dry, and they can occur basically anywhere—**if an area gets rain, it can flood**. They can be caused by anything from extreme amounts of rain to quick melting of ice and snow; **tsunamis** (page 101) or **hurricanes** (page 92); *or even an overeager beaver's dam that caused a river to overflow*. And it doesn't take a ton of water to create a lot of problems—**humans can be knocked over by as little as 6 inches of moving water**.

Some floods, like the **Huang He river floods in China**, are overwhelmingly devastating—those floods in particular **killed approximately 7 million people between 1887 and 1938**, making them some of the most devastating natural disasters in recorded history. In the most destructive flood in 1931, 34,000 square miles of land—*that's almost the size of Indiana*—were completely covered in water, destroying the homes of 80 million people.

SILT HAPPENS

After floodwaters recede, affected areas are usually covered in silt and mud, making cleanup a headache. But Mother Nature also treats floods as an opportunity to pay humans back for their pollution—much like your passive-aggressive roommate putting your dirty dishes in your room, sharp debris, pesticides, untreated sewage and fuel are all commonly left behind.

SUN

Though we've known for quite some time that the sun is essential to life on Earth—just look at the ancient Egyptians, who considered the sun god Ra to be the king of the gods—the sun is also extremely capable of smiting you down where you stand (*or tan*). It's the obvious culprit behind **heat waves** (page 96), but the sun can also take you out in a few other ways.

As anyone who's ever had a sunburn knows, that life-giving star is also capable of literally baking your body. In severe cases, sunburns can even be deadly—in 1999, an 86-year-old Alzheimer's patient was left on an Arizona nursing home patio and sustained a fatal level of sunburn.

Most people won't be killed by one awful sunburn—*but the sun may eventually get you if you soak in enough UV rays over the course of your lifetime*, the prime catalyst for skin cancer. According to the World Health Organization, **about 60,000 people die each year from exposure to the sun**. If you're reading this, though, it's probably too late for you—according to Dr. Anjali Mahto, "Suffering with **one or more blistering sunburns in childhood or adolescence more than doubles your chances of developing melanoma**, which can be potentially fatal."

As soon as you stare directly at the sun, your eyes begin to burn. With enough UV light, cells in your cornea begin to crack and blister, just like a sunburn anywhere else on your body. Keep looking at the sun and you might develop a permanent blind spot in the center of your field of vision, or worse, go completely blind if for some reason you insisted on staring at the sun for prolonged periods. This is still true if you stare at the sun during a solar eclipse—in 1962, a 16-year-old named Louis Tomososki closed his left eye while staring at an eclipse for about 20 seconds, burning a hole in his right retina. In 2017, 70-year-old Tomososki told reporters he could see someone's face but not their nose.

POISONOUS PLANTS

Much like collecting guns or building model rockets, gardening is a hobby that can kill you. There's a flowering plant with sap that can melt your face off, a fruit-bearing tree that could send you into a coma and three-leaved terrors so treacherous there's a *Batman* villain named after one. Sharpen your pruning shears and be ready for a fight.

MONKSHOOD (ACONITUM NAPELLUS)

Also known as wolfsbane, leopard's bane, women's bane, Devil's helmet, blue rocket and conite, **monkshood will almost definitely kill you if you eat it and do not receive medical attention.** This is something humans have known for centuries—according to the University of Cambridge, the highly toxic plant was a favorite choice for **poisoning arrows and spears** in early northern Asian societies. The plant was also put in raw meat as a way to kill wolves and panthers in the 1700s, explaining one of its more common monikers.

All parts of the plant contain the toxin **aconitine**, meaning you shouldn't touch the plant, much less eat it. Unfortunately, its roots look a lot like **horseradish**, *causing the occasional gardener or backpacker to make a fatal mistake.* Ingesting monkshood causes **vomiting, diarrhea, tingling sensations, racing heart beats and blood pressure irregularities**.

Luckily, **you can easily avoid death by monkshood** by not eating any plants you find outside, a homegrown salad from a careless gardener *or making anyone mad enough to poison you.*

HERBAL REMEDY

Your chances of getting poisoned by monkshood are increased if you live in Asia and use herbal medications. The plant can be boiled or steamed to reduce its toxicity, and is then commonly used as a tincture to treat joint and muscle pain. However, less stringent regulations increases the likelihood of getting a fatal dose.

POTATOES

We know what you're thinking: potatoes don't kill you. Potatoes are great. They've been nurturing people for hundreds of years and are pretty much perfect, whether baked, mashed or fried.

However, thanks to their status as a member of the nightshade family, **potatoes can also kill you**. Like other kinds of nightshade, potatoes naturally produce the poisonous compound **solanine**. Usually, a potato contains enough solanine to keep insects from eating them, but nowhere near enough to make a person sick.

Green potatoes are a different story. When potatoes are exposed to warm temperatures and light for prolonged periods, both chlorophyll and solanine increase, making the potato a lot more green—*and a lot more poisonous*. According to Alexander Pavlista, professor of agronomy and horticulture at the University of Nebraska, Lincoln, **16 ounces of green potato** is enough to make a 100-pound person sick. *Guess how much a large baked potato weighs?*

To be fair, **most people would never naturally eat enough green potatoes to die from solanine poisoning**. But to protect yourself against experiencing **extreme vomiting, diarrhea, hallucinations, partial paralysis, being comatose and a possible untimely death**, *store your potatoes in cool, dark places and don't risk eating a green one.*

ELDERBERRY

Like many plants, **elderberries can be useful or deadly to humans**, depending on how they're used. Native Americans used the plant to treat infections, while ancient Egyptians used it to make a salve for burns. There's also evidence to suggest **elderberries improve cold and flu symptoms, fight cancer and protect against UV radiation**.

Then again, eating uncooked or unripe elderberries can cause **nausea, vomiting and diarrhea**. Also, the roots, seeds, leaves and stems all produce **cyanide**, making them unsafe to eat. In 1983, a group of people on a remote "religious/philosophical" retreat in California learned this the hard way after they **made their own juice from freshly picked wild elderberries**—people began vomiting within 15 minutes of drinking the juice and also reported feeling **weak, dizzy, numb and dumb**.

BETEL NUTS

According to BBC, **almost 10 percent of the world's population is addicted is betel nuts**, *the fourth-most popular psychoactive substance most of the western world hasn't heard of*. It's popular in Asia and the Pacific, where you might see people with purple-stained smiles—**a dead giveaway they've been chewing on betel nuts**. Technically the seed of the **Areca catechu**, a kind of palm tree, people often enjoy the nuts as a "**quid**," meaning they've been ground up or sliced and wrapped in lime-coated betel leaves. Eating the nuts makes people feel a burst of energy, **often accompanied by feelings of euphoria**.

If you're wondering why the U.S. hasn't started importing betel nuts, it's because **the FDA has placed them on its Poisonous Plants Database**. *And no, they're not being lame*: chewing betel nuts is also linked to **high rates of oral cancer**, a statistic that probably isn't helped by the fact that many people enjoy their quids garnished with cinnamon, cardamom and tobacco.

CHERRY PITS

The seeds of pretty much any stone fruit, like cherries, apricots, plums and peaches, contain **amygdalin**, a cyanide-like compound. Unfortunately, **amygdalin becomes a cyanide-exact compound when your body digests it.** Specifically, your body produces hydrogen cyanide—the same compound Nazis used in gas chambers. *Neat trick, right?*

While most of those pits are more likely to choke you than poison you, **cherry pits are much more easily swallowed**. That being said, swallowing a pit whole is unlikely to get you sick— **the pit needs to be chewed before being swallowed in order for the amygdalin to be released**. So don't panic, unless you swallow a broken cherry pit, *in which case you should probably panic.*

In the 1950s, cancer researchers patented Laetrile, a purified form of amygdalin. The idea was that the cyanide your body produced would kill cancer cells but not you. While this was a popular alternative treatment in the '60s and '70s, studies have not found any definitive benefits to purposefully turning your body into a cyanide factory. However, *WebMD* does warn that high doses of Laetrile can result in cyanide poisoning and death. But did you really need an internet doctor to tell you that?

BITTER ALMONDS

There are two kinds of almonds: **sweet ones**, like the kind President Obama would famously snack on, and **bitter ones**, *like the kind a horror movie villain would use to poison someone.* **In theory, you could also use sweet almonds in a dastardly manner, as both contain hydrocyanic acid, aka cyanide.** But sweet almonds contain so little cyanide that the average adult would need to eat around 1,150 nuts in one go in order to get poisoned. Bitter almonds, on the other hand, can be about 50 times more potent— **eating just around 50 of them could make you deathly ill**.

If you live in the U.S., you don't have to worry too much about accidentally getting poisonous almond butter—**the sale of raw bitter almonds is illegal**, and the almonds are no longer dangerous after they have been processed. But you shouldn't keep scarfing down any almonds that happen to taste unusually bitter, *as accidents do happen.* In 2014, **Whole Foods recalled one brand of raw almonds** after learning the imported nuts were, in fact, the poisonous kind.

Ingesting bitter almonds comes with some nasty side effects, including dizziness, nausea, vomiting and increased breathing and heart rate. If you eat enough of them, you could lose consciousness, have lung injuries, slowed heart rate and respiratory failure, then die.

Cyanide is so deadly because it denies oxygen to your heart and brain, causing your body to shut down rather quickly. And the smaller you are, the fewer bitter almonds it takes to kill you. In 2013, a 5-year-old boy in Morocco nearly died after eating just 10 of the noxious nuts. His mother brought him to the hospital after he began vomiting and became dizzy, confused and fatigued. He then experienced seizures and fell unconscious. According to a case study, the boy had a "Glasgow Coma Scale at 10"—apparently this means he had a "moderate" coma, but it goes without saying that you never really want to rank on any sort of coma scale. Thankfully, the boy recovered after three hours of oxygen treatment.

RHUBARB LEAF

Don't use a whole rhubarb when baking a strawberry-rhubarb pie. **While the bitter stalk pairs well with sweeter fruits,** *the leaves pair well with hospital visits.* Thanks to their high amounts of oxalic acid, eating a few servings of rhubarb leaves will cause nausea and vomiting—**and, if you eat enough of them, death.**

It takes a lot of bitter rhubarb leaves to make humans sick. But in WWI, **at least one soldier died after the British government recommended eating rhubarb when food supplies were low.** The soldier likely died while having difficulty breathing, a burning sensation in his mouth and throat, nausea and diarrhea. *All in all, it's not a pleasant way to go.*

SMOOTH OPERATOR

You should also probably avoid eating the other end of rhubarb—people in ancient China, Greece and Rome all used the dried roots of rhubarb plants as a laxative.

HONEY

Unless you're an infant (under 12 months old), honey is fine to eat. If you are a baby, *congratulations on your reading skills,* but stay away from all honey—it may contain **botulism spores,** which release a toxin your widdle body is too small to handle.

For the rest of us, **honey is only problematic when bees make it from toxic plants.** This happens a lot on the shore of Turkey's Black Sea, where locals refer to the toxic honey as *deli bal,* or **"mad honey."** Adults can eat this toxic honey in tiny quantities—no more than 1 tablespoon every 24 hours—*and many choose to do so in order to get a sweet high.* Just a bit of mad honey can cause light-headedness and hallucinations.

A lot of mad honey is poisonous. Overdo it and you'll have **low blood pressure, heartbeat irregularities, nausea, numbness, blurred vision and seizures.**

CHILI PEPPER

Jalapeño, scotch bonnet and habanero peppers can all lend a nice kick to your meal, but they won't cause any lasting pain (*unless, of course, you're dumb enough to touch your eye with your capsaicin-covered fingers*).

Still, you might want to rethink those Carolina Reaper wings—when people say those peppers are "deadly hot," they aren't kidding. Carolina Reapers top out at about 2.2 million Scoville heat units—for comparison, habaneros only reach 350,000 heat units. And when capsaicin levels get that high, dinner can go from spicy to scary.

In 2016, one British pub hosted a wing-eating contest using **Carolina Reaper sauce**. Sure enough, many of the contestants wound up in the hospital with **severe cramping, swollen intestines and burnt stomach linings**. One man even complained of being *unable to pee due to spicy urine*. The prize for all this pain? Successfully eating 10 wings and waiting 5 minutes to have a drink afterward was awarded with £9.95, *a refund of the cost of the meal.*

TOO HOT TO HANDLE

In 2008, one 33-year-old died after eating a large amount of hot chili sauce, which he had made for a contest with a friend. After eating a plateful of food covered in the sauce, he went into cardiac arrest later that night.

MOLD

Whether you find it in an old yogurt container or growing on your bathroom tiles, the sight and smell of mold probably grosses you out. Our **natural aversion to furry growths** makes sense—mold is definitely not something you want to eat, and **some types of mold can make you sick through proximity alone**.

While most people wouldn't **voluntarily eat mold**, some may think you're fine if you just cut away the moldy part of your baguette and enjoy the rest. *Those people are wrong and probably have diarrhea all the time*—in soft products, like bread, fruit and cheese, **the mold can send threads throughout the food**, meaning you're still at risk of ingesting all kinds of bacteria, like listeria, salmonella and E. coli.

Mold growing in your home tends to make you sick in other ways. These molds give off **spores that can damage your lungs** if you breathe them in for a long period of time, so clean your shower and use bleach on any suspicious substances. Some types of mold, like ***Stachybotrys chartarum***, can produce mycotoxins that one Michigan State study tied to "*a myriad of respiratory, immunologic and neurologic symptoms.*"

WHAT A FUN GUY

We know what you're thinking—technically, mold is a kind of fungus, which means it's not a plant (or an animal). We're putting it in this section anyway; don't @ us.

GIANT PINE CONE

Pine cones, which children like to slather with peanut butter and seeds to turn into bird feeders, *aren't usually known for their deadly properties*. But some trees, like the **Australian bunya pine**, produce cones the size of a watermelon—**and you don't want one of those suckers falling on your head.**

As one lawsuit from 2014 alleges, that's exactly what happened to a man relaxing in the **San Francisco Maritime National Historic Park,** which had planted these Australian pine trees. **A 16-pound pine cone fell on his head**, immediately knocking him out, bloodying him and **causing brain damage**, according to his lawyer.

Naturally, Australia has been dealing with these trees for quite some time. In 2012, ABC Australia reported that **a 120-year-old bunya pine in Warragul was dropping huge pine cones**, some weighing up to 10 kilograms (*22 pounds*), according to the Baw Baw Council (*local government*). As Mayor Diane Blackwood wisely pointed out, "*So you wouldn't want to be under one, I tell you.*"

GIANT HOGWEED

Found in states across the northern U.S., giant hogweed lives up to its name by reaching towering heights up to 14 feet. The thin green stalks are topped with wide white flowers that can reach 1 to 2 feet across, **and the whole plant is covered in toxic sap that makes your skin unable to protect itself from the sun.** Touching the plant and then being exposed to UV rays results in **severe burns, painful blisters and permanent scarring**.

In one case in Virginia, **a 17-year-old unknowingly covered himself in toxic sap** while chopping down a giant hogweed for his landscaping job. He didn't realize how badly he was burned until he took a shower that evening. As he told *People*: "I started rubbing my face. I thought it was just a little bit of skin at first, *but then big chunks of my face were falling off.*" After two days of treatment at a burn center, **the boy was required to avoid the sun for up to six months.**

CASTOR BEAN

Commonly pressed and made into castor oil, **humans mostly use these beans as a laxative**. And while *WebMD* says there is also "some evidence that a single dose of castor seeds with the outer coat removed (hulled) can work as a contraceptive for up to 8 to 12 months," *we think you should rely on that at your own risk*. Either way, **you'll notice people don't ingest the hulls of these beans**. That's because they're filled with **ricin**, which, as anyone who has watched *Breaking Bad* knows, is a poison that's great for killing your enemies (*or at least trying to*).

Inadvertently swallowing a handful of castor beans will cause a whole host of issues. Vomiting, bloody diarrhea, severe dehydration and seizures are all potential symptoms.

If you were to inhale ricin, you'd also start experiencing symptoms within a few hours: **difficulty breathing, fever, nausea, coughing and tightness in the chest are all signs of being poisoned**, along with excess lung fluids and heavy sweating. Eventually you would have low blood pressure and respiratory failure, killing you. And if you're wondering how this could ever happen, just ask the CDC: It warns that ricin "*could be used to expose people through the air, food or water…if refined into a terrorist or warfare agent.*"

In 2019, one Delaware mom named Jessica Ewing was in the middle of a custody battle and took things a bit too far when she ordered castor beans online, attempted to extract ricin from them and used the substance to spike a chocolate milkshake. Perhaps the most disturbing part of her plan was using her 8-year-old daughter as an unwitting accomplice—Ewing had her daughter give the murderous milkshake to her ex-husband and beg him to drink it. Luckily, this guy knew what his ex was capable of and instead stashed the milkshake in his freezer to be tested. While there wasn't any ricin in the milkshake, it did include another nontoxic substance found in castor beans, which was proof enough for Delaware police to charge Ewing with a felony.

SUICIDE TREE

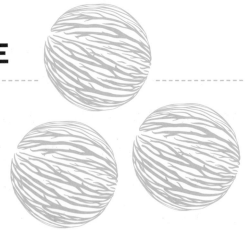

Technically known as ***Cerbera odollam*** (and also known as a **murder tree**), this medium-size tree native to India and southeast Asia boasts some of the most deadly seeds in the world. Laced with the toxic chemical **cerberin**, just one seed is enough to kill an adult human—**and it's conceivable that you could accidentally eat one**, *as they're at the center of the tree's edible fruit.* Sadly, the tree gets its name from the fact that many people choose to eat its deadly seeds on purpose.

SOME LIKE IT HOT

One 2004 study suggests some *Cerbera* suicides may have actually been murders—the seeds are easy to hide in spicy dishes.

Cerbera seeds also have a troublesome history as the poison of choice in **trials by ordeal** in Madagascar, in which alleged witches would be forced to consume the seeds—surviving meant you were innocent, and if you died, ***well, you were a witch anyway and must have deserved the awful stomach pains, diarrhea, vomiting and headache before succumbing to the cerberin.*** About 3,000 Malagasy people died each year until the practice was banned in 1861.

ACKEE

The **national fruit of Jamaica**, ackee is a staple to the island population's diet and popularly eaten alongside codfish. But those who enjoy the fruit need to be careful—**eating ackee before it fully ripens means ingesting a poison called hypoglycin.**

Colloquially known as **Jamaican Vomiting Sickness**, eating hypoglycin causes, well, a lot of vomiting. If untreated, the yacking may also be followed by **convulsions, coma and death**. To avoid this outcome, wait until the fruit turns red and naturally opens, exposing the edible yellow arilli. *And oh, don't eat any of the seeds: Those are toxic too.*

Unfortunately, *it seems that other countries seem to occasionally forget how to handle the poisonous fruit.* In 2001, **at least 44 Haitians died over just six weeks due to ackee poisoning**. According to *IPS News*, the problem reoccurs as the public is unaware of the fruit's dangers and **is more likely to believe the deaths are caused by "supernatural phenomena."**

CASSAVA

You would think a staple food for about 700 million people worldwide wouldn't also be super poisonous. But that's exactly the case with **cassava, a plant that thrives in tropical conditions and requires less human effort per calorie than potatoes**. (And the tubers can be boiled, mashed or fried in much the same way.) The drawback, of course, is **cassava is full of cyanide in its raw, unprocessed state**. Still, its natural toxicity has a silver lining: Growers don't need to worry about pests eating their crops.

Improperly treating cassava can be deadly, especially if you're preparing **bitter cassava** instead of **sweet cassava**. Both varieties contain **hydrogen cyanide**, which keeps your cells from fulfilling the respiration process—*if you're not a science nerd, that means your cells will quickly start to die, meaning you will start to die too.* But bitter cassava contains much more cyanide than its doppelgänger and needs to be processed much more carefully, **making mistaking one tuber for the other a potentially fatal error.**

KIDNEY BEAN

As far as we know, **kidney beans have never been solely responsible for killing anyone**, but they sure might make you wish you were dead if you don't cook them properly. While many beans contain a dangerous toxin called **Phytohaemagglutinin** (which the USDA usually just calls "kidney bean lectin"), they usually don't contain enough to make anyone sick.

Kidney beans, as you've probably surmised, contain a lot of lectin—**their toxicity registers at about 70,000 hau**. But once they're properly prepared, this number goes all the way down to **400 hau**, *meaning the only thing you need to be concerned about is whether they'll make you fart.*

If you're the kind of person who can't boil water, don't try to cook raw kidney beans—**just four to five uncooked beans can make you sick**. Symptoms include extreme gastrointestinal pain with nausea and vomiting, plus diarrhea. To avoid this, **boil your beans for at least 10 minutes**, or avoid any risk altogether and buy them canned. And **don't put unboiled raw beans in a slow cooker**, which will never come up to a boil.

NUTMEG

Nutmeg has **a surprisingly long and sordid history** beyond its use in pumpkin spice lattes. As far back as the 12th century, **nutmeg has been snorted or eaten in large amounts to create a hallucinogenic high**, and in the 1500s it was taken to induce miscarriages.

In the '60s, nutmeg reemerged as a party drug (*whether people knew nutmeg got you high or they were simply snorting everything they could find is unknown*). In the 1963 article "Nutmeg Intoxication" from the *New England Journal of Medicine*, health professionals wrote that while the spice "is much cheaper for use and probably less dangerous than the habit-forming heroin, it must be stated that **it is not free from danger and may cause death**." Still, you would have to ingest about 2 teaspoons of nutmeg to risk death.

CASHEW

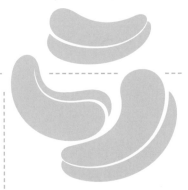

If you've never seen a cashew plant, take a moment to look it up. **They appear somewhat creepy**, *with the cashew seeds actually growing outside the fruit like some sort of tumor.* But aside from the fact that it looks extremely unappetizing, **there's a reason cashew fruits aren't sold whole** so you can enjoy both the fruit and the seed: **Unprocessed, the cashews you know and love are extremely toxic**.

Raw cashews have two layers of hard shells, *with different kinds of acid layered between them* that will burn your hands if you take them off without protective gloves. After shelling, the nuts still contain **urushiol**—the same resin that makes poison ivy (page 130) give you a rash—**and must be roasted to become edible**.

If you do decide to take a crack at preparing your own cashews, make sure to roast them outdoors, as even the smoke created from roasting cashews is toxic and can irritate your lungs "to a life-threatening degree," according to *Parade*.

POISON IVY

Like the infamous Batman *villain, poison ivy is toxic to touch.* Along with all the other members of the ***Toxicodendron*** genus, including poison sumac and poison oak, **poison ivy is covered in a resin called urushiol that will almost definitely give you an itchy rash**. A lucky 20 to 40 percent of the population isn't affected by urushiol, *but we don't suggest touching poison ivy to see if you're one of them.*

If you've ever had the displeasure of brushing up against some poison ivy, **you know the rashes they leave behind are barely soothed by calamine**, regardless of what the internet says. Your skin may become red, swollen and itchy within a few hours or up to five days after coming in contact with urushiol. **Eventually the rash will blister, become crusty and flake off**, *but it could take up to five weeks before you heal completely.*

Most poison ivy rashes can be treated at home, but the Mayo Clinic suggests contacting your doctor if your reaction affects your eyes, mouth or genitals; your blisters are oozing pus; or if you have a fever greater than 100 degrees F.

(DON'T) LET IT BURN

Whatever you do, don't burn poison ivy in order to remove it from your backyard. Inhaling the smoke could give you a rash on the lining of your lungs, which is extremely painful and could easily kill you.

According to some folk medical practices, eating very small pieces of poison ivy in order to build up a tolerance to urushiol can make you immune to the toxic resin. This might not be as stupid as it seems—in a 2006 study, small amounts of poison ivy extract placed under the tongue gave patients a "much higher threshold for allergic skin reactions," according to *WebMD*. Of course, this is wildly different from just snipping a piece of poison ivy and tossing it down the hatch. But some "natural health" blogs advise doing just that. For obvious reasons, like the potential of the ivy causing a rash in your throat that would make it impossible to breathe, this is not advised by the medical community.

131

NETTLE

Most people are familiar with **the aptly named stinging nettle**, which is famous for its **formic acid-tipped trichomes**, aka stinging hairs. *Like most acids, you don't want this touching your skin.* Just brushing up against one of these plants will give you a burning sensation and an itchy rash that will last for the next day. If this doesn't sound too bad, it's because it's really not—**as long as you don't get too many nettle stings**.

There's no record of anyone having ever died from touching stinging nettle (*Urtica dioica*), but its close cousin, **tree nettle (*Urtica ferox*) is a different story**. As another kind of nettle, *U. ferox* are covered in the same stinging hairs. They also grow in dense patches up to about 6 feet tall, *and it would be a bad idea to forge your way through a patch of them.*

Unfortunately, barging through tree nettle is exactly what two young men did in New Zealand in 1961, where nettle trees are abundant. Both men were stung multiple times on their limbs, and within an hour one of them began to struggle with walking and breathing, then went blind before dying five hours later at a hospital. His friend had similar symptoms, but thankfully recovered.

GYMPIE-GYMPIE

Yet another member of the Urticaceae family, gympie-gympie, **or stinging trees**, grow in Australian rainforests in Queensland and northern New South Wales. **But this tree has a much worse reputation than regular nettles**. According to entomologist and ecologist Marina Hurley, "Being stung is the worst kind of pain you can imagine—*like being burnt with hot acid and electrocuted at the same time*." She would know, having developed an allergy to the tree while studying it as a postgraduate student— **and taking precautions like protective particle masks and welding gloves didn't keep her from getting stung**.

The gympie-gympie tree has long been known as a terror. In 1866, one road surveyor reported that his horse "**was stung, got mad and died within two hours**." Other accounts include horses being in **so much pain that they threw themselves from cliffs**; forestry workers getting outrageously drunk in order to numb the pain; and **at least one military officer shooting himself** *—he made the horrible mistake of utilizing one of the tree's leaves for "toilet purposes."*

WAX ON, WAX OFF

If you ever have the misfortune to be stung by this tree, don't try to pluck the needles out with tweezers—they're too fine. Instead use hot wax to rip them all out.

MISTLETOE

There are two kinds of mistletoe: ***Phoradendron serotinum***, the American species, and ***Viscum album***, its European counterpart. The American kind is commonly used to weirdly pressure people into kissing around the holidays; the European variety has a long history in traditional medicine as **a treatment for headaches, seizures and arthritis**. You shouldn't eat either one, but if you're ever forced to pick one or the other, go with American mistletoe—*you might get a stomachache, but you probably won't die.*

In one study of 1,754 cases of American mistletoe ingestion, **there were no fatalities and just a handful of people experienced "gastrointestinal upset."** The more potent European mistletoe, however, could definitely keep you from seeing the New Year— according to the National Capital Poison Center, **both poisonings and deaths have occurred after eating European mistletoe.**

UNDER THE BIRD POOP

Mistletoe is a parasitic plant that lives on trees, and it especially likes to grow where birds have recently relieved themselves. In fact, the name comes from the Anglo-Saxon *mistel*, meaning "dung," and *tan*, meaning "twig"—over time, *misteltan* evolved into mistletoe.

POINSETTIA

Like mistletoe, this holiday plant gets a bad rap but is not especially deadly, to you or your pets—**even the ASPCA states poinsettias are "overrated in toxicity."** According to *Snopes*, the rumor likely started in 1919 when a child's death was incorrectly attributed to eating poinsettia leaves. Apparently, it would take eating more than a pound of poinsettia leaves to endanger a 50-pound person. Aside from the fact that that's about 500 leaves, the bitter taste is enough to prevent consumption.

Still, *unless you enjoy cleaning vomit out of your carpets*, you should make sure your kids and animals don't snack on poinsettia leaves. The plant has an "**irritant sap**" that can cause tummy aches, barfing and diarrhea. It's also advised to look but not touch, as **some gardeners have gotten rashes from handling poinsettia plants**.

HAIRY HEIMLICH

According to James C. Schmidt, a horticulturist at the University of Illinois, poinsettias can still pose another threat to curious cats: "Reports of convulsions in cats are due to choking on the fibrous plant, not poisoning."

HOLLY BERRY

Rounding out the holiday hazards are holly berries. **Its sharp-pointed green leaves are enough to deter those** *who don't want to slice up their tongue while chewing on them*, but the festive red berries are more deceptive, so you should decorate with faux boughs if you have any pets or children in the house.

According to one study, holly berries aren't deadly but may ruin your holiday if you eat too many of them—**and if you're a child, that means as few as five berries**. Some people seem to be more heavily affected by **saponin**, the berries' toxin, than others. In one case of identical twins each eating a "handful" of holly berries, **one experienced drowsiness and vomited 40 times in just six hours,** while the other was granted *the Christmas miracle of only throwing up five times and remained alert.*

POISON HEMLOCK

Though **poison hemlock isn't native to North America**, it was brought over in the 1800s for decorative purposes—and with the ability to produce 1,000 seeds each season, **the pretty-yet-poisonous plant quickly spread all over the continent**.

According to the National Capital Poison Center, this makes the plant especially problematic for the livestock industry, **as animals in pastures don't tend to discriminate between hemlock and hay**. To be fair, humans aren't always great at picking out hemlock, either: It looks very similar to many other edible plants, such as **wild parsnip, wild celery and wild chervil**, *making foraging lunch a bit of a gamble*.

SOCRATIC METHOD

In 399 B.C., Socrates was sentenced to death and served as his own executioner by drinking a cup of poison hemlock. On top of causing a painful death, the drink must have smelled terrible—poison hemlock smells like mouse urine when crushed.

If you do ingest poison hemlock, you're in for a terrible time as the plant's poison wreaks havoc on your nervous system, *first stimulating and then paralyzing your nerve endings*. Vomiting, difficulty moving, trembling, rapid breathing, salivation, peeing yourself, feeling nauseous, **having convulsions, falling into a coma and dying** are all common side effects.

FOXGLOVE

Technically called **Digitalis purpurea**, the beautiful foxglove is favored in the medical community for making heart medication—the drug is rather effective in strengthening contractions of the heart muscle. Of course, you don't need to be a doctor to understand that **it's not advised to take heart medication when you don't need it**, *which in turn makes eating any part of a foxglove plant or making tea from its leaves a risky endeavor.*

According to the U.S. National Library of Medicine, foxglove poisoning usually occurs when people eat any part of the plant, or from "**sucking the flowers**." (*We're not sure why you would do that, but if you're thinking about it, don't.*) Symptoms of poisoning include collapsing, low blood pressure, blurred vision, hives, diarrhea, stomach pain and weakness. **If you're being slowly poisoned over a long period of time**, you're also likely to experience hallucinations, see halos around objects and have loss of appetite.

OVERTHROW, ITALIAN-STYLE

Cangrande I della Scala, an Italian warlord, died just four days after conquering Treviso in 1329. Though his contemporaries blamed it on drinking from a polluted spring, historians have long suspected murder. This theory got a lot stronger after Cangrande's corpse was exhumed in 2004 and researchers were able to perform an autopsy on his body, revealing toxic concentrations of two chemical compounds produced by foxglove, plus pollen grains from the poisonous plant in his stool.

MANCHINEEL TREE

In case you haven't gathered as much by now, *eating fruits you find in the wild and don't recognize is a Bad Idea*. Nothing quite exhibits this bit of wisdom like the manchineel tree, **which seems to exist purely to kill people**—its fruit is nicknamed *la manzanilla de la muerte*, or "**the little apple of death**."

According to one account of biting into its fruit, the taste is "pleasantly sweet," **but it's all downhill from there**. "Moments later we noticed a **strange peppery feeling** in our mouths, which gradually progressed to a **burning, tearing sensation and tightness of the throat**," wrote radiologist Nicola Strickland in 2000. Her condition worsened until she could barely swallow food and was in "excruciating pain," but luckily the symptoms subsided over the next eight hours.

Even just touching the tree is dangerous, as it's covered in **toxic sap that causes burn-like blisters on your skin** and can temporarily blind you if it gets in your eyes.

OLEANDER

According to the University of Florida, oleander *"may have a bit of a bad-girl reputation, but it is a truly beautiful addition to the Florida landscape."* This questionable commendation comes before a disclaimer against eating any part of the oleander plant, which is highly toxic. **Irregular heartbeat, blurred vision, diarrhea, nausea, vomiting, depression, fainting and hives** are just a few of the side effects listed for those who have ingested oleander.

If you insist on keeping oleander in your garden—*apparently it's great for beach-front homes, as it's "tolerant of sea spray"*—make sure to place it somewhere kids and pets won't be tempted to eat it. And **don't burn any fallen or pruned branches**, as the smoke will be toxic and can cause respiratory issues.

AZALEA

Azaleas are **technically a type of rhododendron**, which are the culprits behind "mad honey" (page 120). That means **ingesting their leaves, nectar or flowers is not a great idea**, though not as dangerous as eating honey made from their nectar, in which the toxins are more concentrated.

Unfortunately, people sometimes **confuse azalea plants for honeysuckle and slurp on the former's nectar**. In most cases, the symptoms are fairly mild: *A bit of mouth irritation, nausea and vomiting will keep you from making that mistake again.* But if you keep chomping on the rest of the plant, you could experience **burning in the mouth, abdominal pain and progressive paralysis** of your limbs.

CALL A PURR-AMEDIC

While small amounts of azalea aren't advised for anyone, they're especially toxic to cats. If your cat likes to chew on plants, keep this out of your garden—it can cause cardiovascular collapse, coma and death.

DEADLY NIGHTSHADE

Perhaps **the most famous poisonous plant of them all**, deadly nightshade is known for having been used to kill countless people throughout history. While ancient Romans liked to use the plant to **make especially lethal arrows with poison tips**, it was probably used in the most effective manner by Scotland's King Duncan I, **who served liquid nightshade to an army of Danish enemies during a truce**. This killed them all, and likely created a scene that would have felt at home in *Game of Thrones*: an entire army dealing with **vomiting, blurred vision, hallucinations, delirium, agitation, coma and convulsions**—all common in nightshade poisonings—before finally succumbing to death.

Deadly nightshade was particularly preferred as a method of poison **because of the potential to build up a tolerance to it**. Spies and taste-testers *(and probably Westley from The Princess Bride)* would ingest small amounts of the plant over time, **giving them the ability to "prove" a drink was safe to consume**.

If you have dreams of building up a tolerance to one of the most toxic plants on the planet, take it very slowly. Just **two nightshade berries can kill a child**, and **10 to 20 can send an adult to their grave**. If you overdo it and can't go to the hospital for some reason, **drink a large glass of warm vinegar or a mixture of water and mustard**, which could neutralize the toxins—*no promises, though!*

FATAL FAD

This plant is also known as belladonna ("beautiful woman") because historically, Venetian women used its oil to dilate their pupils, ostensibly making themselves more attractive.

In 2017, the FDA recalled Hyland's Homeopathic Teething Tablets for mislabeling the amount of belladonna alkaloids found in the product. While the use of belladonna in medicine isn't necessarily an issue, using too much of it certainly is—as the old adage goes, the dose makes the poison. The product had been linked to the deaths of 10 children and even more cases of seizures or vomiting. In other sad news, Hyland spokesperson Mary C. Borneman told CNN that 24 people lost their jobs after the product was discontinued. Still, the American Academy of Pediatrics suggests avoiding any product with belladonna (or probably any other poison) to help your teething child—instead, try a firm rubber teething ring, or tell your kid that pain builds character.

JIMSON WEED

Also known as **devil's trumpet, mad apple and stink weed**, jimson weed is commonly found throughout the continental U.S. All parts of the plant are poisonous, *though it can also be used to get high*, as British soldiers found out in 1676. After dining on boiled jimson weed, the soldiers were sent to stop the **Rebellion of Bacon** but were soon waylaid by their own shenanigans.

According to Robert Beverly's *The History and Present State of Virginia*, written in 1705, "they turned natural fools upon it for several days: one would blow up a feather in the air; another would dart straws at it with much fury; and another, stark naked, was sitting up in a corner like a monkey, grinning and making mows [grimaces] at them."

While that sounds like a grand old time, *things become a lot less fun if you overdo it with the old devil's trumpet*. Early signs of poisoning include **depression, diarrhea and frequent urination**, among other symptoms. In fatal cases, victims may have a **weak pulse, lowered body temperature, convulsions and could fall into a coma before death**.

AGAVE

While this desert plant is famous for its place in **mescal and tequila**, eating or even touching the unprocessed plant sap is not advised— in fact, **Mexican Tarahumara people would tip their hunting arrows in the toxic sap**.

If you do touch the sap, you'll immediately feel pain and a burning sensation as blisters begin to develop on your skin. Eating the sap can lead to even worse outcomes, as it can give you severe kidney and liver damage.

Because the plant looks almost exactly like *aloe vera, a harmless plant that ironically would be great for treating blisters*, it can be extremely easy to confuse the two. One vlogger known as Zhang did just that in 2017, **when she bit into an agave plant during a live broadcast she called "Aloe Vera Feast."** According to *Shanghaiist*, Zhang realized something was wrong after "just one bite made her mouth go numb and her throat feel like it was on fire." Luckily, though she **broke out in blisters and rashes and needed to have her stomach pumped**, she survived the mishap.

ROSARY PEA

This plant's seeds were commonly used as rosary beads, *which may be useful if you need to pray for help after accidentally ingesting one*. Rosary pea seeds contain the natural poison **abrin**, making them wildly toxic.

If you **swallow one of the seeds without chewing**, you'll probably be OK. But if someone were to feed you the crushed seeds, *you should start saying some Hail Marys on your way to the hospital*.

In 2008, a 27-year-old man arrived at a hospital after having **intentionally swallowed 10 ground seeds**, resulting in vomiting and "liquid black stools." After treatment with activated charcoal, he was spared symptoms such as **bloody urine; hallucinations; seizures; failure of the liver, spleen and kidneys; and death.**

DOLL'S EYES

Berries from doll's eyes are decidedly creepy-looking. Clusters of **white berries with black, pupil-like dots** grow on bright-red stems, *making it seem as though you're being watched from all angles*. They're also super poisonous.

Though birds can eat these berries, **most mammals, including humans, can't**. Burning of the mouth and throat would happen very quickly, followed by **salivation, headache, extreme stomach cramps, hallucinations and dizziness**.

Doll's eyes also contains **cardiogenic toxins** that act as a sedative on cardiac muscle tissue. In other words, they can make you go into **cardiac arrest (*aka your heart stops beating*)**—which will definitely kill you if it's not fixed stat.

TRICK OR TREAT

This plant has flowers in earlier seasons—the eyeball-like berries don't come in until fall, just in time for Halloween.

DAFFODIL

According to the National Capital Poison Center, **people eating daffodils isn't as unusual as you might think**. Young children are attracted to the bright pops of color, and the **plant's bulbs look a lot like onions**, leading adults to make some unfortunate mistakes.

If you do forage for vegetables, remember that **daffodil bulbs don't smell like onions and won't make you cry when you cut into them**. They will, however, give you **nausea, diarrhea and abdominal pain, and probably make you throw up**. This is because the toxic chemical **lycorine** is found in all parts of the plant and is most concentrated in the bulb.

The bulb also has tiny, needle-like chemicals called oxalates, which irritate your skin and cause severe burning of the lips, tongue and throat if swallowed.

TOXIC TREATMENT

In ancient times, daffodils were used to treat various ailments. According to the book *Pharmacodynamic Basis of Herbal Medicine*, this was risky: Bulb extracts were sometimes used as anti-inflammatory agents for open wounds, but this could also result in "staggering, numbness of the whole nervous system and paralysis of the heart."

WHITE SNAKEROOT

Native to North America, white snakeroot is a weed that **grows just about anywhere**. This is problematic for farmers, whose livestock eat the plant and ingest large amounts of the toxin **tremetol**. If the animal eats enough tremetol, **they may develop "trembles" and die**.

The situation becomes a lot worse for people when cows and other livestock eat just enough snakeroot to **pass the toxin onto us via their milk and meat**—this was a huge problem in the early 1800s, when "**milk sickness**" killed many people, including Abraham Lincoln's mother, Nancy Hanks Lincoln. The poisoning presented a lot like the flu, with symptoms such as **vague pains, weakness, muscle stiffness and vomiting,** *until the person falls into a coma and dies*.

Today you don't need to worry too much about **toxic milk**, as commercial dairy is usually **pooled from different areas**, keeping potential toxin levels low. But if you have your own cow, *maybe don't drink its milk if it's been shaking violently*.

CHINABERRY TREE

All parts of this tree are toxic, but people do ingest it—in **traditional Chinese medicine**, parts of the Chinaberry tree are used as an antiparasitic and antifungal agent, though people **make tea from the bark** and drink it for almost any ailment.

According to Chinese medical texts, **six to nine berries or 30 to 40 seeds** must be ingested for the average person to be sick. Poisoning could have **gastrointestinal, respiratory, cardiovascular or neurological** effects (*so pretty much everything*), and death can occur in severe cases.

PARTY FOWL

While the berries are toxic to mammals, birds enjoy them because of the "drunken state" it puts them in. You can tell if a bird has hit the berries too hard if it's having a hard time getting off the ground.

146

MUSHROOMS

Like mold (page 122), mushrooms are **technically a kind of fungus and therefore not a plant**, but we're going to talk about them here anyway. While some mushrooms are perfectly fine to eat—*go ahead and enjoy that portobello burger*—some are so poisonous they've earned nicknames like "**the death angel**."

This doesn't bode well for people who like to **pick and eat wild mushrooms**: It's very difficult to identify them, **cooking them doesn't make them safe** and their symptoms can be extreme. Some poisonous mushrooms cause the **classics: vomiting and diarrhea or hallucinations and coma**. But other kinds creep up on you with **no effects except for liver damage**, *which can be deadly if you don't know you need a new liver until it's too late.*

MUSHROOM MAXIM

As the old saying goes, there are old mushroom hunters and there are bold mushroom hunters, but there are no old, bold mushroom hunters.

EUROPEAN YEW

Like a lot of plants in this section, almost every part of *Taxus baccata*, aka the European yew, is poisonous. The poison taxane is present in the wood itself, the thin green leaves and the seeds in the berries—but not the flesh of the berries themselves.

Unlike a lot of plants in this section, **there are often few symptoms of being poisoned by European yew**—if you unknowingly eat a few of its seeds, *you may think you're completely fine until you drop dead a few hours later*. If you are one of the rare people who experiences symptoms beforehand, they would likely include **trembling, weakness, a weak pulse and sudden death**.

Because the berries themselves are not poisonous, **you may be lucky and survive if you don't chew thoroughly before swallowing them**. In one case, a 19-month-old child survived after eating the berries—the seeds were found undigested in his stool, meaning **he likely would not have been so lucky if he had properly chewed his food**.

AND IF YEW DON'T KNOW, NOW YEW KNOW

Around 77 A.D., Pliny the Elder wrote that vessels made from yew wood killed those who drank wine from them.

CALADIUM

All parts of the caladium plant (**aka angel wings, elephant's ear and heart of Jesus**) are poisonous. Native to the Amazon, the broad-leafed plants are now **grown all over the U.S.**— people like them because they grow well in the shade and come in many colorful varieties; *they just have the minor drawback of potentially poisoning your pet or any curious kid that likes to put random objects in their mouth.*

Like daffodils (page 145), caladium contains **toxic, needle-like crystals known as oxalates**. If you were to chew on a caladium leaf, you'd quickly experience **burning, blistering and swelling of your lips, mouth and tongue**; sometimes this is severe enough to prevent normal speaking and swallowing. You're also likely to become **nauseous, followed by diarrhea and vomiting**.

Even just touching the plant's sap can irritate your skin—gloves are recommended for planting these toxic tubers. The U.S. National Library of Medicine also warns against getting any of this plant's sap in your eyes—unsurprisingly, something that burns your skin can also burn your eyeballs.

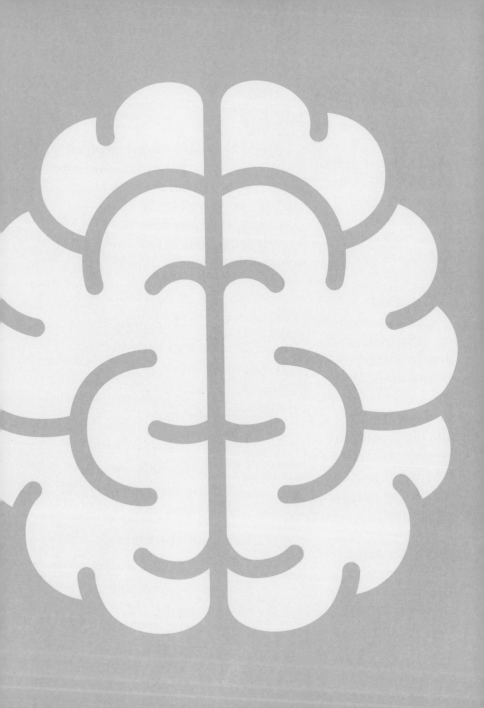

DEADLY DISEASES

Perhaps you live a blessed life and survived that lionfish encounter, your bout with ringworm, a hurricane or two and that time you accidentally wiped your forehead with poison oak. Too bad there's still a good chance you'll meet your end from a bad case of diarrhea. Wash your hands, carry some antibacterial gel and give up kissing forever. It's your only hope.

NECROTIZING FASCIITIS

If you have a fever, nausea or dizziness soon after an injury or surgery, it could just be the stomach flu. **Or, if you're super unlucky (and not great at using soap), it could be flesh-eating bacteria.**

Necrotizing fasciitis can be caused by different strains of bacteria, but the CDC suggests **group A *Streptococcus*** is the most common. The infection is rare but can be innocuous, entering the body through an everyday cut you shrugged off. When this bacteria infects the deep fascia, the layer of soft tissue between the muscles and skin, **it spreads throughout the body.**

Gross symptoms include ulcers, black spots and blisters on the skin, and pus and oozing of the infected area. So if that cut has become incredibly painful and redness is spreading quickly, you should probably see a doctor right away — *your chances of living are a lot better if you receive antibiotics and surgery as soon as possible.*

CHOLERA

If you've never read *Love in the Time of Cholera* by Gabriel García Márquez, rest assured the book doesn't do a deep dive on the specifics associated with dying from this decidedly disgusting disease, *perhaps because there's something objectively unromantic about what is effectively "death by diarrhea."*

Cholera is specifically caused by a bacteria called ***Vibrio cholerae***, which loves to hang out in contaminated water. **If you live in a country with modern sewage and water treatment systems (and you don't eat undercooked shellfish, another known carrier of the bacteria), you're probably fine.** In fact, you might even be fine if you do ingest some cholera, though you will shed the bacteria in your stool for the next one to two weeks, meaning you can contaminate others if you don't wash your hands after using the bathroom.

If you were to be infected by cholera, you would lose up to a quart of fluid in just an hour via some very watery diarrhea. According to the Mayo Clinic, **"Diarrhea due to cholera often has a pale, milky appearance that resembles water in which rice has been rinsed (rice-water stool)."** So definitely be on the lookout for that because the resulting dehydration and loss of electrolytes can cause death within three hours if left untreated.

DENGUE

This mosquito-borne viral disease is like the flu from hell, complete with **severe pain, rash and bleeding from the gums and nose.** It can also worsen into a condition called **dengue hemorrhagic fever (DHF)**.

DHF includes vomiting, severe abdominal pain and difficulty breathing, plus your small blood vessels become "leaky." *And in case you didn't know, they should not be leaky.* This can lead to circulatory failure, shock and then death if the circulatory failure isn't fixed. **There is no specific treatment for dengue.**

SAVE YOUR ASS

There's no vaccine for dengue, so your best bet against contracting it (apart from not living in an area where these or any other disease-carrying mosquitoes fly around) is to eliminate standing water, which is where female mosquitoes like to lay eggs. Don't forget not-so-obvious sources of water like flower vases, which the CDC recommends emptying and cleaning at least once per week to remove any eggs and larvae.

PLAGUE

It wasn't until plague's most recent global outbreak, **which lasted from 1860 until 1959**, that scientists finally pinpointed the cause of the infamous infection: *Yersinia pestis*, a bacteria mostly found in rodents and their fleas. **When those fleas hopped from rats to cats to the unwashed masses, all hell broke loose**.

For more than 1,000 years, plague was Mother Nature's favorite way to keep humans from taking over. **The Plague of Justinian**, the earliest well-documented pandemic, started in 542 A.D. According to *National Geographic*, it's estimated that **plague killed about 10,000 people per day in Constantinople**, and by the time the bacterial infection disappeared nearly two centuries later, Europe's population had been halved. Even more infamous was the Black Death, *that pesky medieval outbreak you might have heard of*. That one stuck around for centuries and killed around 25 million people. Fun side effects before death included **gangrene, pus-filled glands that often erupted, and—wait for it—dissolving lungs**. There are three forms of plague:

Septicemic plague affects the bloodstream. People catch this either from fleas or from plague-infected body matter (*read: saliva; blood; poo; bloody poo*).

Bubonic plague is the best-known and most common form of the disease. Its name refers to the **buboes: swollen lymph nodes the size of chicken eggs**, that appear on the groin, armpit or neck of the infected.

Pneumonic plague is an advanced form of bubonic plague and **the most infectious form of the disease**. At this stage it can be passed from person to person via coughed-up air droplets.

If you thought plague was gone, think again. One recent outbreak was in 2017 in Madagascar, resulting in 2,300 cases. According to the CDC, an average of seven plague cases are reported in the U.S. each year, and 1,000 to 2,000 cases are reported globally, though actual cases are likely higher. Luckily, plague is usually not fatal if treated with antibiotics, so if you notice you've got a lump the size of a chicken egg near your groin, maybe get that checked out.

HANTAVIRUS

Mostly **spread by rodents**, hantaviruses are a family of viruses that can make people sick in a lot of different ways. In the Americas, hantaviruses are usually carried by deceptively cute mice and cause **hantavirus pulmonary syndrome (HPS)**, a respiratory disease that has a decent chance of killing you—**about 38 percent of people who contract the illness die**, according to the CDC.

After coming in contact with the **fresh saliva, droppings or urine of an infected rodent**, the disease incubates for somewhere between one and eight weeks. Then, victims experience early symptoms such as fatigue, fever, muscle aches, headaches, chills, vomiting, nausea and abdominal pain. Essentially, *you'll probably think you have the flu until late symptoms set in four to 10 days later*, with coughing and shortness of breath indicating your lungs are filling with fluid.

If you've been playing with mice—especially deer mice, cotton rats, rice rats or white-footed mice—and have these symptoms, get yourself to a hospital. There is no formal treatment for hantavirus, but those in intensive care units have a better shot at living.

LISTERIA

What do queso fresco, smoked fish and hot dogs have in common? They're all common breeding grounds for **listeria, a bacteria that can cause listeriosis**. While most people don't have to worry too much about this bacteria, **Listeria monocytogenes** can cause severe infections in older adults, newborns and anyone else with a weak immune system. If you fall into any of these groups, **your bloodstream and brain are at the greatest risk**—listeria can cause sepsis, meningitis or encephalitis, *all of which should thoroughly ruin your appetite for undercooked hot dogs and old deli meat.*

Pregnant women also need to be wary of foods that may be contaminated with listeria, as **the bacteria is especially harmful to fetuses**—it can cause miscarriages, stillbirths and newborn deaths.

SPOILED SALADS

Vegans also need to be wary of listeria, as produce—especially raw sprouts, celery and melons—is another favorite place for the bacteria to grow.

RABIES

As WHO makes clear with a poster of a young boy holding an adorable puppy, **it's extremely easy to pick up rabies**. Bites from infected domestic dogs are the main cause of rabies infections in most countries, **especially in Asia and Africa where dogs aren't as commonly vaccinated**. Of course, it is possible to contract rabies if you're bitten or scratched by any infected animal—**in America, the No. 1 culprits are bats**.

If you contract rabies, it's vital to get treatment ASAP. Early symptoms may seem like the flu, followed by **cerebral dysfunction such as anxiety, agitation and confusion**. Once you begin to show clinical symptoms of rabies, including **delirium, weird behavior, fear of water, hallucinations and insomnia**, you might as well be put down—*just like Old Yeller, it's too late for you.*

DANCING PLAGUE

Between 1374 and 1518, a handful of "dancing plagues" afflicted people living near Strasbourg, France. The best-documented of these was the final outbreak in 1518. It began with a woman named **Frau Troffea**, who began dancing on the street outside her home on July 14, **and did not stop until she collapsed hours later**. But the next morning she was at it again, and the plague seemed contagious—within a week, some 30 more people were dancing with her, all ignoring their own hunger, thirst and bloodied feet. **Within a month, 400 people were boogying until they just couldn't boogie no more, meaning they literally dropped dead**. (*And according to etchings by Hendrik Hondius, they did not look good doing it.*)

At the time people believed the plague was **caused by either "hot blood" or Saint Vitus,** *the patron saint of dancers and epileptics who happened to have a shrine just 30 miles away*. While some believe the dancing was caused by **ergot, a mold that causes jerking and hallucinations**, historian John Waller pointed out that the mold also restricts blood flow to the extremities, **making weeks of dancing impossible**.

Instead, **Waller suggests the dancing was psychosomatic**—people in the Middle Ages were anguished by **poor harvests, syphilis and political instability**, and expressed their pain through dance because they believed St. Vitus was doing it to them. *Or maybe, like The Go-Go's, they had "the beat."*

MAD COW DISEASE

In what is probably a butcher's worst nightmare, mad cow disease, aka **bovine spongiform encephalopathy or BSE**, occurs when an unknown agent starts killing cow brain cells, creating *sponge-like holes*. You may not realize the cow is infected right away—the disease can incubate for years. But within a year of activation, *the cow's brain will start to resemble Swiss cheese*, causing it to behave oddly and then die.

Though it doesn't seem smart to eat meat from a brain-diseased cow, **food industries initially decided it was probably fine and ground it up anyway.** As it turned out, it was definitely not fine, as whatever caused the BSE caused something called **vCJD (variant Creutzfeldt-Jakob disease)** in humans.

Like BSE, vCJD will definitely kill you if you have it, but may incubate for years. Initially, symptoms include **depression and loss of coordination**. In later stages, patients will have **dementia and brain abnormalities**. Though vCJD is incredibly rare, you can minimize your risk by skipping "*mechanically recovered meat and head meat*," which is found in burgers, sausages and meat pies.

EBOLA

Though scientists aren't sure where the Ebola virus came from *(their best guess is bats)*, they do know it's **a highly deadly disease that can be highly difficult to contain.** Spread by the blood or body fluids of someone who is infected, health-care workers often get infected themselves when caring for patients. It also does not bode well for areas like **Guinea, Sierra Leone and Liberia**, where tradition demands that their dead be washed and dressed by hand—**any saliva, blood, feces, vomit or even sweat from the recently deceased could spread the virus**.

After contracting the disease, **symptoms show up within three weeks**. Though EVD presents much like the flu, with the disturbing addition of **unexplained bruising or bleeding**, it's much more deadly: The average fatality rate is around 50 percent.

SCURVY

Infamous for afflicting pirates, scurvy is a nasty disease caused by not getting enough vitamin C. If you didn't know, you can't make vitamin C on your own, and you need it for things like making neurotransmitters, strengthening your skin, blood vessels and bones, healing wounds, absorbing iron and a bunch of other things that help keep you more human than zombie.

As the condition worsens, things start to look pretty bleak: **bulging eyes; swollen, bleeding gums; loose teeth; scaly skin; bleeding into joints and muscles; slow-healing wounds**—*and horrifyingly, the opening of previously healed scars*—are all late symptoms of scurvy. Untreated, scurvy can eventually lead to a **heart attack, anemia or death**.

If you don't ingest any vitamin C, **scurvy will set in within about four weeks**. Initially, it will seem like the flu: fatigue, loss of appetite, diarrhea, fever and painful joints and muscles are all common, *though the "pinpoint" bleeding around your hair follicles should give you pause*.

UP IN SMOKE

Cigarettes are terrible for a lot of reasons (see page 212), and you can add increased risk of scurvy to the list—the extra stress smoking puts on your body means you need more vitamin C.

In 2019, scientists found that King Louis IX may not have died of plague or dysentery, as they had previously thought, but of scurvy. Apparently, Louis IX was a bit of a picky eater, which isn't ideal when you're also a crusader. By choosing to survive on fish and apparently ignoring the local produce in Tunis, the area he was busy besieging, the king developed a severe case of scurvy. The disease plagued his army as well—according to medieval chronicler Jean de Joinville: "Our army suffered from gum necrosis and the barbers had to cut the necrotizing tissue in order to allow the men to chew the meat and swallow. And it was a pity to hear the soldiers shouting and crying like women in labor when their gums were cut." #yikes.

HIV

Despite any rumors you may have heard, **HIV/AIDS didn't come from human interactions with monkeys—** *but it probably did come from apes.* Scientists believe the virus was first transmitted to humans when **humans in Central Africa hunted infected chimpanzees for their meat**, and the simian immunodeficiency virus mutated into human immunodeficiency virus.

Though science has come a long way in controlling HIV when it's caught early on, **the virus can still be devastating**. HIV attacks the immune system, destroying T cells and making you highly susceptible to other infections and diseases. If untreated, **HIV will eventually progress to AIDS** (acquired immunodeficiency syndrome). In this final stage, the victim may experience chills, sweats, fever, swollen lymph glands, weight loss and weakness, and they are at extreme risk for developing an "**opportunistic infection**," such as salmonella (page 168), toxoplasmosis (page 72) or tuberculosis (page 172).

GET THEE TO A CLINIC

If you have unprotected sex or share a needle, you could have (and therefore spread) HIV for a decade or longer and have no idea. The only way to know for sure is to get tested.

YELLOW FEVER

Transmitted from person to person via mosquito, you're at high risk of getting yellow fever if you're in Central Africa or South America. About a week after being bitten by a carrier mosquito, you'll experience **severe headache, back pain, nausea and vomiting,** *and may remain fatigued for several months after "recovering."*

In some people, **yellow fever gets much worse.** After a short remission, you might enter the "**toxic phase.**" Jaundice (*aka yellowing of the eyes and skin, hence the name*), dark urine, stomach pain and vomiting, plus bleeding from the mouth, nose, eyes or stomach can all occur, **ending with organ failure and death in about 50 percent of those who enter this stage.**

(DON'T) SPREAD THE LOVE

If you think you have yellow fever, see a doctor (obviously) and do your best to keep from getting any more mosquito bites for at least five days—you don't want the disease being passed onto others.

BRAINERD DIARRHEA

Though it's not quite the Mall of America or the statue of Mary Tyler Moore, Minnesota can add "*the first place where an unexplained, weeks-long diarrhea epidemic broke out*" to its claims to fame. Named for the town where it first affected 122 people in 1983, Brainerd diarrhea presents with **acute onset watery diarrhea lasting for four weeks or longer, and it has no apparent cause.**

On top of having **three or more loose stools per day**, victims may experience gas, mild stomach cramps and fatigue. Unfortunately, without knowing what's causing the disease, **we lack an effective treatment.** Brainerd diarrhea eventually resolves on its own, but **symptoms can last a year or more,** and "*typically come and go.*"

SMALLPOX

Though it's since been eradicated* (score 1 for vaccines), smallpox was a great way to get scarred, go blind or be killed from around the 3rd century B.C. until 1977, when the last person on record naturally acquired smallpox.

Prior to 1977, however, smallpox, **aka the variola virus**, was a true terror. The disease was very similar to chicken pox—*think rashes, sores filled with virus-y fluid, scabs that eventually fall off*—**but with a much higher mortality rate**. Spread all too easily by coughing and sneezing and even inanimate objects like bedsheets contaminated by fluids or fallen scabs, **smallpox killed about 30 percent of those who were infected by it**.

BUT WHY?

*Though the disease has been "eradicated," it hasn't exactly been wiped off the Earth. Two labs, one in Atlanta and one in Koltsovo, Russia, still store the variola virus. Apparently, scientists still need to perform research. If you're worried about a breakout, rest assured that no lab has accidentally leaked the virus out of an air duct and killed someone since 1978 (that we know of).

CANCER

As the **second-leading cause of death in the United States**, cancer seems to be the reward most of us can expect for living more than half a century. **One in four deaths in the U.S. are from the disease**, and the majority of those people develop the disease after they turn 65.

At its most basic, **cancer is a group of cells in your body growing out of control**, often resulting in a tumor that can get in the way of the rest of your organs trying to function. It can form anywhere—**such as your lungs, colon, skin or blood**—and spread all over your body.

Overindulging in **cigarettes, alcohol, cured meats, red meats, processed foods and sweets** all raise your risk of cancer. Of course, it might be in your DNA, *in which case all the kale chips in the world won't save you.*

GANGRENE

While technically more of a side effect than a disease or bacteria unto itself, **gangrene is both nauseating and deadly enough to deserve its own writeup.** Having gangrene literally means **parts of your body are dying**, usually because of a bacterial infection or lack of blood flow.

If gangrene affects your skin, you'll be able to tell by the **discoloration (ranging anywhere from blue to red to black), the fluid-filled blisters, sores leaking nasty-smelling discharge and a clear line between the dying parts and the healthy parts**. If you have gangrene internally, it will be much less obvious—swollen, painful tissue and a low-grade fever are the only clues you'll get.

If you don't treat your gangrene quickly enough, **scarring** (*not so bad*) and **amputation of your now-dead limbs** (*pretty bad*) are both possibilities. If the gangrene is caused by bacteria and spreads to your organs, **it can very well be fatal** (*super bad*).

LEPROSY

Also known as **Hansen's disease**, leprosy is easily managed and can even be cured with proper treatment. Unfortunately, *"proper treatment" isn't shipping lepers off to live in their own colonies without medicine*, **so historically humans with leprosy haven't fared very well**.

Brought on by the bacteria ***Mycobacterium leprae*** attacking your nerves, eyes, skin and lining of your nose, leprosy usually causes it victims to be **unable to feel pain or sense touch**. And though being numb won't technically kill you, *not realizing that cut on the bottom of your foot is horribly infected (or even there) certainly could*. In severe cases, victims' hands and feet can become paralyzed, **and your body may even "reabsorb" the cartilage in your toes and fingers**, making them much shorter.

As if all that weren't horrifying enough, leprosy can also result in **blindness, corneal ulcers, loss of eyebrows and "saddle-nose deformity,"** which means the bridge of your nose collapses. So if you develop **lighter or darker skin with loss of feeling**, see your doctor ASAP—a few rounds of antibiotics will keep your digits from shrinking.

ALOHA, LEPERS

If you like depressing-yet-beautiful vacations, a visit to the former Kalaupapa leper colony on the island of Molokai, Hawaii, is perfect for you. Now a refuge for the last residents who were sent to live (and die) there, you can fly, hike or ride a mule to see where 8,000 people perished.

ANTHRAX

Though it's rare to naturally come across anthrax bacteria in the U.S.—*you're (slightly) more likely to be sent an envelope of* Bacillus anthracis *by someone who you've really, really pissed off*—**it's naturally occurring in soil around the world**, including Central and South America, the Caribbean, southern and eastern Europe, sub-Saharan Africa, and central and southwestern Asia.

When anthrax spores enter your body, whether directly through an open wound, by ingesting the meat of an infected animal or via inhalation, you're in for a bad time. If you're ever playing a literal game of "Would you rather," go for anthrax via open wound—all you'll get is an ugly but painless sore, and you probably won't die if you get treatment.

Eating an anthrax burger will result in **nausea, vomiting, bloody diarrhea and a swollen neck**, but even that is better than inhaling anthrax, **which is usually fatal even with treatment**. Before death, you'll probably have flu-like symptoms, nausea, begin coughing up blood and potentially get **meningitis**, aka inflammation of the brain and spinal cord.

SALMONELLA

Salmonella, aka the most compelling argument for not ordering your chicken medium-rare, is a bacteria that plagues about 1.2 million Americans each year. Those with healthy immune systems have an awful few days of diarrhea, abdominal cramps and fever, but recover without needing anything more than Pedialyte.

But occasionally, **salmonella can be a much more serious infection**. The bacteria causes around **450 deaths each year in the U.S.**—severe illness is much more common if you're especially old, young or have a weakened immune system.

While it's pretty much common knowledge to avoid salmonella by not eating food that has sat out at unsafe temperatures, **you should also be wary around animals**. The CDC recommends always washing your hands after petting animals, not putting your hands in your mouth after petting animals *and not kissing any chickens, turtles or lizards*.

CLAIM TO DIARRHEA-INDUCING FAME

Salmonella bacteria was first discovered by an American scientist named—wait for it—Dr. Salmon.

E. COLI

More formally known as *Escherichia coli*, this family of bacteria is commonly found in the intestines of both animals and people. Most strains help keep your intestinal tract running smoothly, **but six pathotypes are "diarrheagenic,"** *meaning they cause a different kind of "runs."*

Aside from making you rush to the bathroom, **certain strains of E. coli can also cause urinary tract infections, pneumonia and respiratory issues, among other illnesses**. The most common form of E. coli infection in the U.S. is **Shiga toxin-producing E. coli (STEC)**, which results in severe stomach cramps, bloody diarrhea and vomiting.

People who ingest STEC usually get well within five to seven days, **but up to 10 percent may develop hemolytic uremic syndrome**, a life-threatening complication that, among other serious issues, **causes your kidneys to stop working**. Most recover from HUS within a few weeks, but some will have permanent damage or die— *so wash your lettuce, people.*

HEPATITIS A–E

Hepatitis A, B, C, D and E are all different viruses which can mess up your liver, leading to **fibrosis** (scarring), **cirrhosis** (more bad scarring) or **liver cancer**.

Hep A often results in two months of **fatigue, stomach pain, nausea and jaundice**—and that's one of the more mild forms of the virus. Types B and C are the worst offenders, **causing hundreds of millions of people to suffer from chronic disease**. While Hep B is mostly transmitted sexually, you get Hep C from being exposed to infected blood. *Count that as just one more reason not to share needles.*

Perhaps most disgustingly, Hep A and E are both transmitted by **"ingestion of fecal matter,"** *which is the CDC's polite way of saying "eating poop."* This usually occurs via unsanitary water, and while there's a vaccination for Hep A, there isn't currently one for Hep C, **so stick to bottled water when traveling**.

MENINGITIS

As *WebMD* helpfully explains, meningitis affects the **meninges**, the membranes covering your brain and spinal cord—and "*you or your children can catch it.*" Swelling of the meninges can be brought on by bacteria or a virus, or more rarely by things like **fungi, drug allergies and cancer**.

Regardless of how you develop meningitis, **it can get very scary, very quickly**. According to the Mayo Clinic, early symptoms include sudden **high fever, stiff neck, a strong headache that feels "different than normal," confusion and seizures**, to name a few.

GYM, TAN, HOSPITAL

In 2019, three Jersey Shore beaches temporarily shut down after dangerous levels of "fecal bacteria" known to cause a host of issues, including meningitis, showed up in water samples. Somehow, we're not surprised.

If you have meningitis and you decide it's not worth a trip to the hospital, things will probably get a lot worse. More serious seizures, memory difficulty, hearing loss, learning difficulties, issues walking, kidney failure and death are all potential side effects.

GROUP A STREPTOCOCCUS

Though it's **most commonly known for causing strep throat**—something you probably had as a child and recovered from just fine with some antibiotics—group A strep can also cause some **much more serious, life-threatening diseases**.

When group A strep begins making toxins inside your body, it gives you a rash—**the telltale sign of scarlet fever**. Like strep throat, scarlet fever is usually mild, even though your rash may keep peeling for a few weeks. But both can take a turn for the worse if not properly treated. You may get **pockets of pus around your tonsils, pneumonia, arthritis, post-streptococcal glomerulonephritis** (*a rare kidney disease you definitely do not want to have*) **and rheumatic fever** (*a heart disease you also do not want to have*).

Need one more reason to **always wash your hands** and not breathe too close to coughing people? Consider that **group A strep is believed to be the most common cause of necrotizing fasciitis** (page 152), aka flesh-eating bacteria.

PNEUMONIA

This **particularly nasty infection of the lungs** is caused by all sorts of reasons—bacteria, fungi, chicken pox and measles are all potential sources, *though good old group A strep (see above) is the most common culprit*.

If you have pneumonia, **the air sacs in your lungs are filled with fluid or pus**. This results in coughing up said pus, plus a fever, chills and difficulty breathing (*which is something you generally want to do easily*). While pneumonia isn't always more concerning than the flu, **it can become deadly**.

Complications from pneumonia can lead to difficulty getting enough oxygen, a lung abscess or bacteria in your bloodstream, **spreading the bacteria to your organs**. Plus, if fluid builds up between your lungs and chest cavity and gets infected, *you better hope there's a doctor nearby to drain it with a chest tube or remove it with surgery*.

TUBERCULOSIS

Also known as TB or consumption, tuberculosis can develop when you breathe in TB bacteria, giving it the opportunity to set up shop in your lungs. From there the bacteria can grow, giving you an awful cough, pain in your chest and probably making you cough up blood or sputum, aka phlegm from the depths of your lungs.

Once TB bacteria is in your lungs and growing, it's free to move about your body. Untreated, tuberculosis can spread to places such as your **kidney, spine or brain**. And while TB is treatable, people can easily make it worse if they don't carefully follow their doctor's instructions—if you don't finish the prescription or take the drugs correctly, *you could essentially create super-bacteria that is much harder to kill.*

While vaccines and better health overall have radically decreased the prevalence of TB in the U.S.—**the disease killed one out of every seven people in the early 1900s**—outbreaks still occur. You may even have latent TB and have no idea—while your currently healthy immune system suppresses the bacteria, **getting sick with something else later, like diabetes or cancer, could cause the TB to develop**.

WORLDWIDE KILLER

While TB isn't common in the U.S., it's one of the top 10 causes of death globally.

TB bacteria has been terrorizing humans for centuries, earning nicknames such as "the white death," "the great white plague" and "the graveyard cough." In the early 20th century, those with "consumption" were often placed in sanatoriums, where fresh air and bed rest were the main methods of treatment. But as historian Sheila Rothman explained, no amount of fresh air could protect patients from the infamous wasting disease: "However much the sanatorium resembled other institutions, it had one unique feature—the omnipresence of the shadow of death." On the plus side, the infected were at least kept from spreading the disease further.

FATAL FAMILIAL INSOMNIA

Yet another prion disease, fatal familial insomnia is a **degenerative brain disorder**—and as you probably surmised from the word "familial," *you can thank your parents if you happen to get this rare genetic disease.*

Initially, those with FFI have symptoms of **mild insomnia**, or being unable to sleep. As the disease worsens and you get less and less sleep, **you slowly lose the ability to control your body**. This happens because abnormal prions are building up in the thalamus of your brain, causing you to lose neurons. Unsurprisingly, **this affects a lot of obvious brain functions**—you may have symptoms such as unintended weight loss, forgetfulness, confusion and problems concentrating. And though you're not sleeping, *you will almost definitely feel like you're having a nightmare*, since hallucinations, panic attacks, phobias, paranoia and dementia are all common side effects.

As your brain continues to deteriorate—and you get less and less sleep—symptoms such as double vision, jerky eye movements, slurred speech, and trouble swallowing and coordinating voluntary movements can all occur. Eventually, the disease leads to coma and death.

DYING TO SLEEP

If you're wondering why these people don't pop some sleeping pills, it's because they don't work on FFI patients. In fact, doctors don't have any effective treatment for FFI.

COPD

Whether it's caused by **emphysema, chronic bronchitis or something else,** chronic obstructive pulmonary disease (COPD) makes it difficult for you to breathe. *And as you already know, breathing is pretty important to this whole "life" thing you're probably enjoying.*

Before COPD kills you (*and as the third leading cause of death in the U.S. in 2014, that's a real possibility*), it can make your life barely worth living. Along with unsurprising side effects such as **frequent wheezing and coughing, shortness of breath and excess phlegm/mucus/sputum,** COPD can make you unable to work, eat out, go to group events or "**[get] together with friends,**" according to the CDC. *Apparently, portable oxygen tanks aren't really all that portable.*

If you want to avoid becoming someone who sits inside all day chained to an oxygen tank, **the best thing you can do is not smoke,** followed by avoiding other air pollutants and respiratory infections.

CREUTZFELDT-JAKOB DISEASE

Not to be confused with variant CJD, which is related to mad cow disease (page 159), classic CJD is another prion disease that will definitely kill you if you have it. Luckily, **getting CJD is like winning the lottery**—it occurs in just one out of every million people.

Terrifyingly, **doctors don't know why the "sponge-like lesion in your brain" disease occurs in 85 percent of cases, nor how to treat it.** According to the CDC, "CJD occurs as a sporadic disease with no recognizable pattern of transmission," *which is basically science-speak for "IDK, man."*

Symptoms of CJD include **walking difficulties, sudden jerky movements, rapid onset dementia and potentially visual disturbances.** It's a pretty scary way to go, but if it's any consolation, it will all be over relatively quickly—*once you see these signs, you'll probably die within the year.*

DIABETES

If you have diabetes, *aka the disease that seems to specifically have it out for Americans*, it means your body is unable to break down the sugars in your bloodstream and turn them into energy. Over time, **having too much sugar in your blood** (and not enough energy in your body) can lead to some pretty nasty side effects—according to the CDC, **diabetes is the leading cause of lower-limb amputations, adult blindness and kidney failure in the U.S.**

Incredibly, though type 2 diabetes is completely preventable by maintaining a healthy weight, eating sensibly and exercising at least three times per week— basically everything Michelle Obama begged Americans to do as FLOTUS—it makes up about 90 percent of diabetes cases. The disease is the seventh leading cause of death in the U.S., and the number of diagnosed adults has more than doubled in the past two decades.

Though the disease is extremely prevalent in the U.S., **about 25 percent of diabetics are undiagnosed**. If you lose weight without trying, are often thirsty or hungry, have blurry vision, tingling or numb extremities, have more infections than usual and slow-healing sores, *you're both long overdue for a doctor's visit and a likely candidate for diabetes treatment.*

NOT MY TYPE

If you have type 1 diabetes, all the broccoli and running in the world won't save you—daily doses of insulin are necessary to survive.

NOMA

Technically a type of gangrene (see page 165), noma, aka cancrum oris, is an infection that destroys the mucus membranes in your mouth and slowly breaks down tissues in the cheeks and lips before moving onto the bones around your mouth, effectively turning you into the *Dark Knight* version of Two-Face.

Doctors don't know exactly what causes noma, though it **"may be due to a certain kind of bacteria,"** according to the U.S. National Library of Medicine. What we do know is the infection starts out as ulcers in your gums and linings of your cheeks. The ulcers then develop a *"foul-smelling drainage,"* and the infection rapidly spreads to your skin, **killing your lip and cheek tissue before moving on to your bones**.

If you're considering becoming a bubble boy to avoid this disease, rest assured you probably don't need to worry about this one—tragically, noma **most often affects malnourished children between the ages of 2 and 5 in sub-Saharan Africa**. Then again, WHO reports that "sporadic cases" have been "recently reported" in the U.S., Mexico and Europe.

LOOK OUT BELOW

Noma can also affect genital skin—when the disease spreads there, it's known as noma pudendi.

INFLUENZA

Though many of the diseases in this book shrug off "flu-like symptoms" as being minor, **influenza can be fatal**. It's especially dangerous if you're over 65 or under 5 years old, but it's potentially deadly for anyone, **regardless of your age or health**.

Some flu seasons are worse than others. According to the CDC, **U.S. flu deaths per year have fluctuated between 3,000 and 49,000 since the mid 1970s.** Though the flu could theoretically kill you on its own via breathing problems and dehydration, most die from more serious complications, including **bacterial pneumonia, sepsis or infections in the heart or brain**.

In children, signs of the flu becoming life-threatening include **bluish skin, trouble breathing, intense irritability, fever with a rash and not waking up**. In adults, emergency symptoms include **confusion, persistent throwing up, sudden dizziness, chest pain or pressure, and difficulty breathing**. If you or your kids show any of these symptoms, get to the hospital ASAP.

YOU ONLY GET ONE SHOT

Your best chance to fight the flu is to get a flu shot—the CDC suggests everyone 6 months and older do so each year.

In 1918, the pandemic known as the Spanish flu killed up to 50 million people, including about 675,000 Americans. Doctors did not have any effective treatments for the rapidly mutating virus, which had the ability to take down healthy people with incredible ease—some victims were dead within a matter of hours after developing symptoms, having turned blue after suffocating from fluid-filled lungs. In fact, the flu was so devastating that the average life expectancy of Americans decreased by 12 years, and more U.S. soldiers died from the flu than were killed in battle during World War I that year.

BLASTOCYSTOSIS

Though the itty-bitty organism *Blastocystis hominis* is found throughout the world, scientists aren't exactly sure what it is—in the past, it's been classified as a yeast, fungi or sporozoan protozoa, among other things. Currently, scientists consider it to be a stramenopile, a group that includes things like water molds and slime nets.

Now that we've cleared that up, *let's get to something else scientists are only pretty sure about*: They think these microscopic organisms cause a disease called **Blastocystosis**. While many people have Blastocystis in their intestines and show no symptoms, your infection could present with **abdominal pain, anal itching, weight loss, diarrhea, constipation and excess gas**. If you do get Blastocystis in your system, you better hope you don't have any symptoms—**the organisms could stay inside you for weeks, months or years**.

DRINK UP

Blastocystosis probably won't be what does you in, but if it did, it would likely be from dehydration.

CORONARY ARTERY DISEASE

If you need help stepping away from bacon cheeseburgers, **just think about all the plaque building up in your heart**, giving you coronary artery disease (CAD). The plaque, which is made up of **cholesterol deposits**, clogs up your arteries and makes it difficult for blood to pass through. *And if your heart isn't getting enough blood, you're not long for this world.*

One of the most common symptoms of CAD is **angina, *which sounds funny but is decidedly not*** — angina is the pain you feel in your chest when your heart muscle doesn't get enough blood. With enough time, **CAD will weaken your heart muscle, which can result in irregular heartbeat or heart failure.** In fact, some people don't know they have CAD until they have a heart attack.

WEST NILE VIRUS

Carried by everyone's favorite insect, the mosquito, *West Nile virus usually isn't a big deal until it really, really is.* While about 80 percent of people who get bitten by an infected mosquito don't develop any symptoms, some people do get a pretty harsh fever. Symptoms include **headache, joint pain, diarrhea, rash and vomiting.** The virus usually isn't fatal, but you could feel fatigued for months after you've "recovered."

In incredibly rare cases — about 1 in every 150 people — **West Nile virus can be nightmare-inducing.** If you're one of these wildly unlucky people, the virus will affect your central nervous system, causing **encephalitis** (inflammation of the brain) or **meningitis** (inflammation of the membranes around your spinal cord and brain). *Though this isn't a guaranteed death sentence,* **about 10 percent of people who get these side effects die.**

BYE BYE BIRDIE

If you notice an unusual amount of dead crows and jays in your area, it could be a sign of West Nile virus—they're especially susceptible to the disease.

BALANTIDIASIS

If you've accidentally (*or intentionally*) ingested food or water contaminated with feces, **there's a whole lot of ways it can make you sick**. One of these ways is if the contaminated food also contained **cysts infected with *Balantidium coli*.**

While it's entirely possible to drink some *Balantidium coli*–infested poop water and feel no symptoms, some people will feel symptoms such as **weight loss, stomach pain, vomiting, nausea and nonstop diarrhea.** More serious complications include dysentery (*your intestine becoming infested, resulting in bloody, mucus-filled feces*) and, if you don't get treatment, colon perforation.

While this disease is thankfully rare in the U.S.—it's more common in tropical and subtropical regions—the CDC still recommends you avoid it by following good hygiene practices. This includes washing all produce before eating it, even the kinds with removable skin, and washing your hands after using the bathroom or changing a diaper.

THIS LITTLE PIGGY WENT TO THE BATHROOM

According to the CDC, balantidiasis is more common in people who work in areas where pigs are raised.

MIDDLE EAST RESPIRATORY SYNDROME

MERS is a kind of coronavirus—*we haven't looked this up, but we're guessing this name has nothing to do with the beer*. Still, like most Mexican lagers, coronaviruses are usually pretty mild, and most people will have them at some point in their lifetime. **MERS is not like most other coronaviruses**, however.

While some people with MERS may have a minor infection, **around 35 percent of MERS patients die from the virus**—symptoms before death include diarrhea, vomiting, nausea, pneumonia and kidney failure.

To avoid MERS, follow standard hygiene precautions, and also avoid camels and their byproducts, **as scientists have found MERS in camels from multiple countries**. Do not touch them, eat undercooked camel meat, drink raw camel milk or—*just in case you were thinking about it*—drink raw camel urine.

TRACHOMA

Caused by the bacterium *Chlamydia trachomatis*, **trachoma is an infectious eye disease that can leave you blind**. The bacteria is transferred by things like direct contact, shared towels and flies that come into contact with the eyes or nose of someone who is already infected—*if you needed another reason not to bring back the 2013 eyeball licking trend, this is it*.

While the bacteria is easily treated, **places lacking water and sanitation are particularly susceptible**. If untreated, trachoma infections can leave the insides of your eyelids severely scarred, **eventually causing the eyelid to turn inward**. *And if you don't get surgery to fix your eyelashes stabbing your own eyes and scratching your cornea*, you will be in a lot of pain and eventually go blind—at that point, **there is no way to return your sight**.

THE EYES HAVE IT

Despite the fact that trachoma is highly preventable by regularly washing your hands and face, about 8 million people have sight problems due to the disease.

SEVERE ACUTE RESPIRATORY SYNDROME

Commonly known as SARS, **this viral respiratory sickness is caused by a coronavirus**, just like MERS (page 183). As far as doctors know, no one has been infected with SARS since the 2003 global outbreak was contained—*and we should all hope it stays that way.*

According to the World Health Organization, SARS infected 8,098 people that year, 774 of whom died. The disease started out with a high fever, followed by body aches and headaches. Somewhere between 10 and 20 percent of people experience diarrhea with SARS, and most victims develop pneumonia. In the worst cases, victims also suffered from respiratory, heart or liver failure, leading to death.

What made SARS so disturbing was the fact that **we had no effective treatment for a disease that was highly contagious**— every time an infected person coughed, sneezed or even spoke, the virus dispersed via droplets in the air. The first case was reported in China in November 2002, and **the highly contagious disease spread to more than 24 countries in Asia, Europe, North America and South America within a year**.

GONORRHEA

Like many other STDs, *gonorrhea is known for its disturbing symptoms.* If you have a penis, these could include a **burning sensation when you urinate, painful or swollen testicles and white, yellow or green discharge.** Women's symptoms are easier to confuse for other infections, and include the same **pain when peeing, bleeding between periods and increased vaginal discharge.**

Both sexes are also at risk for **infections in their rectums,** which could present with **soreness, anal itching, painful poops, discharge and bleeding.**

If you're sexually active and you don't get tested, you may have gonorrhea and have no idea—the disease is often asymptomatic. While that sounds preferable to the horrible symptoms described here, it's better to have a heads up before the infection spreads and causes further complications. On top of pain in your pelvis, abdomen or testicles, gonorrhea can also spread to your joints or blood, which could potentially kill you.

EVERYBODY CLAP YOUR HANDS

Linguists think this disease may have been nicknamed "the clap" for a few reasons: from the Old French *clapier*, meaning "brothel"; from the Old English *clappan*, meaning "to beat or throb"; or from an old treatment method that involved clapping hard on one's penis to attempt to expel the discharge.

SYPHILIS

As anyone who's taken middle school health class knows, syphilis is one of the more infamous STDs and is commonly spread when people **come in contact with a sore during vaginal, anal or oral sex**. In pre-penicillin days it ran rampant, **eventually leaving large swaths of the population blind, disfigured or insane**.

The infection is usually divided into stages. In stage one, a person usually has **round, firm and painless sores around the site of their infection**. In stage two, people also develop **skin rashes, fever and swollen lymph nodes**. Because both of these stages are pretty mild—you may not even notice the rashes if they're faint—**people may not realize they have syphilis before they move on to the third stage**, where there are no noticeable signs or symptoms.

While all this sounds relatively minor, **it's possible to develop neurosyphilis at any stage of the infection if you don't get treatment**. If this happens, you could have a hard time controlling your muscle movements, become paralyzed, feel numb or contract dementia. **And if you develop ocular syphilis, you could become blind.**

ONE MORE THING

It's also possible to wind up with tertiary syphilis, which usually pops up 10 to 30 years after your initial infection. If this happens to you, the disease will damage your internal organs, probably killing you.

Historians have long suspected William Shakespeare had syphilis, pointing to his signature as evidence—in his later years, it showed an obvious tremor, which would suggest he was taking mercury as treatment for the infection. And according to John Ross, M.D., "Shakespeare's knowledge of syphilis is clinically precise," suggesting that we interpret the line "Love's fire heats water" in Sonnet 154 as a reference to burning pee. Shakespeare also referred to the infection multiple times in his works, writing about the "pox," the "malady of France," the "infinite malady" and the "hoar leprosy." Wethinks the gentleman doth obsess too much.

PERSONAL FAILINGS

Sometimes the deadliest threats we face are written in our genes. You might have bones that break like twigs, a desire to cut off your limbs, the inability to set foot in the sunlight or a tendency to bleed to death from a simple papercut. Congratulations: You're a walking disaster. Thanks, Mom and Dad. But there's good news: We all die from something—at least the way you croak will be interesting.

HOLDING IN A SNEEZE

Generally, being polite is great. And holding your nose and covering your mouth as you sneeze, especially during something like a wedding, seems like a polite thing to do. But it's also impolite to rupture the back of your throat and require immediate medical attention because you tried to hold in a sneeze. *After all, nothing ruins a wedding faster than the arrival of EMTs.*

Just ask the 34-year-old British man who could hardly speak or swallow after inadvertently putting a hole in his throat in 2018. According to *The Telegraph*, doctors also heard **"strange popping and crackling sounds"** that **"extended from his neck all the way down to his rib cage"** while examining him.

If this sounds far-fetched, it's probably because you don't know just how powerful sneezes are—**some experts believe sneezes can travel out of your body at up to 100 miles per hour, which is a lot of pressure to trap inside your ear, nose and throat.**

Doctors later warned the public that keeping yourself from sneezing can cause conditions ranging in severity from perforated eardrums and air getting trapped in your chest between your lungs, to even rupturing your brain and causing an aneurysm. Other cases of people holding in sneezes have resulted in pulled muscles, facial nerve damage and cracked ribs.

So next time you have to sneeze, **just let it out.** You'll be saving yourself an awful lot of risk, and *you just might get a blessing for your trouble.*

DYING FROM LAUGHTER

Despite what that wooden sign in your aunt's living room says, laughter isn't always the best medicine. In fact, like most things in life, **too much of it can kill you.**

Usually, people who die from laughter also have another condition. **For asthmatics, laughing can trigger an attack or cause a collapsed lung.** And those with cataplexy, a condition similar to narcolepsy, can suddenly collapse and lose their muscle strength during a fit of laughter.

Too much laughter can also be dangerous for those with an **underlying heart condition**. Case in point: British man Alex Mitchell, who in 1975 found an episode of *The Goodies* so hilarious he laughed for 30 minutes straight, aggravating his genetic heart condition and causing him to die from heart failure. According to Mitchell's wife, he had one final *"tremendous belly laugh, slumped on the settee and died."* On the bright side, it sounds like a pleasant way to go.

BURSTING A BLADDER

Usually, people will pee themselves before becoming so full of urine that their bladder literally bursts. It's much more likely if you've had major surgery, radiation or have had your bladder surgically reconstructed. If your bladder does burst, **it's incredibly painful and causes urine to seep into your abdomen** (where you obviously don't want urine to be).

But in some rare cases, it does seem possible to hold it until you literally burst. Such was the case with 16th century astronomer Tycho Brahe, who, it's believed, refused to leave a royal banquet to relieve himself out of politeness, **causing his bladder to rupture and become infected**.

Bursting your bladder is also much more likely if you're **drunk and on a boat.** In 2015, a 24-year-old in Maine had a lot of beer and then broke the seal in a very unfortunate way when he dove into a lake, tearing a hole in his bladder. Dr. Bradley Gill, a urologist at the Cleveland Clinic, likened the scenario to *"throwing a water balloon on the sidewalk."*

BOREDOM

If you've ever complained you were "dying of boredom," you may have been right. According to a study from University College London, there's a correlation between boredom and an early death—in fact, bored people are twice as likely to die from heart disease or stroke.

The study began in the mid-'80s, when researchers asked 7,524 civil servants about their boredom levels. Those who reported high levels of boredom were 40 percent more likely to be dead when researchers checked back in with them in 2009; apparently, *not being fulfilled in your work and social life is a big reason people turn to unhealthy habits such as drinking and smoking.* Thanks to the study, we now also know that people in menial jobs are more likely to be bored.

The coauthor of the study, Martin Shipley, gave this helpful advice to those who are suffering from boredom: *"It is important that people who have dull jobs find outside interests to keep boredom at bay, rather than turn to drinking or smoking."* In other words, as your mom probably told you, "Only boring people are bored."

NEED FOR SPEED

Driving while bored can also be a recipe for disaster. A 2012 study found that bored drivers were more likely to try to derive thrills from tailgating, speeding or daydreaming behind the wheel, all of which obviously increase the chance of an accident.

FEAR

If you think you're about to face immediate danger, your body will go into what scientists refer to as **"fight-or-flight mode."** Adrenaline rushes into your system, causing your muscles to tense, your blood vessels to constrict, and your heart rate and blood pressure to go up, all of which prepares your body to fight—or run—for your life.

Unfortunately, if your body overdoes it with the adrenaline, it can have the opposite of its intended effect. In other words, instead of saving you, it could kill you. Technically called stress cardiomyopathy, the rush of adrenaline could cause "acute, sudden heart failure [in people who] were perfectly healthy an hour earlier," according to Ilan Wittstein, a cardiologist at Baltimore's Johns Hopkins Hospital.

You can even be held responsible if you happen to scare someone to death. In one case in 2008 in North Carolina, a bank robber broke into a woman's home while hiding from the cops. Though he didn't touch the woman, the break-in terrified her enough to trigger a heart attack, ending her life—and adding a murder charge to the robber's rap sheet.

EMOTIONAL KEELING

According to Martin A. Samuels, chairman of the neurology department at Brigham and Women's Hospital in Boston, any strong emotion could have a similar effect to being scared to death. As he told *Scientific American*, "There was a case of a golfer who hit a hole in one, turned to his partner and said, 'I can die now'—and then he dropped dead."

ALLERGIES

Having allergies is kind of like being born with a defect—for no real reason, your body insists that a harmless food or other foreign substance, such as pet dander, peanuts or pollen, is incredibly dangerous. To combat the supposed "dangers" of the substance, your body reacts by inflaming your skin, airways, sinuses or digestive system. At best, the reactions are unnecessary and unpleasant, and *at worst, they are unnecessarily life-threatening*.

Usually, the worst allergic response you can have is anaphylaxis. This reaction is most common with food allergies and insect stings. **Symptoms include loss of consciousness, extreme shortness of breath, a drop in blood pressure, light-headedness, skin rash, nausea, vomiting and a rapid, weak pulse.** If you think you or someone else is anaphylactic, get medical help right away—the reaction can cause you to go into shock and die.

COLD URTICARIA

While it's annoying to have to pass on eating anything made in the vicinity of peanuts, having cold urticaria means you should probably move south. **For people with this allergy, staying in the cold means getting some nasty hives**.

If your body can't handle the cold, you'll develop hives on any skin that was exposed to less-than-toasty temps—and they'll get worse as your skin warms up again. You also wouldn't be able to enjoy ice cream or even hold a particularly cold drink, as *swelling of the lips from consuming cold things and swollen hands from holding chilly objects* are both common.

In severe cases of cold urticaria, forgetting your scarf can be a death sentence. Your entire body could go into anaphylaxis, or your tongue and throat could swell, making breathing a difficult prospect. According to the Mayo Clinic, people are most likely to have these extreme reactions if they do something really crazy, like go for an icy swim.

AQUAGENIC URTICARIA

If there's anything more ridiculous than being allergic to the cold, it's being allergic to water—and yet, for some poor souls with aquagenic urticaria, that's exactly their lot in life.

According to the Genetic and Rare Diseases Information Center, the condition is **more likely to affect women and crops up around the onset of puberty**. If you have this extremely rare allergy, *any skin contact with water of any temperature will cause you to break out in hives,* usually on the upper half of your body. The hives may or may not be itchy and will usually fade within an hour.

Because it's insane to *live in fear of getting rained on or taking a shower*, those with aquagenic urticaria live in our 70-percent-water world with the liberal use of antihistamines and creams that can create a barrier between their skin and water. Other treatments that have had some success are **ultraviolet light therapy and omalizumab,** an injectable asthma medication.

H_2NO

People with this allergy don't get their recommended eight glasses of water per day, and usually ingest a lot of produce with high water content and diet sodas to help make up for it. As one Utah teen with the condition told *People* in 2015, "I'm told that someday my throat might swell when I drink water, but if there's one thing I've learned since getting this, it's that we all have things to deal with in life."

Personal Failings

WALKING CORPSE SYNDROME

Also known as Cotard's syndrome, *this is a disorder that makes some people believe they are already dead.* Or at least, that their brains are. Shockingly, at least one case study shows that these patients may be right—kind of.

In 2012, a 48-year-old went to his doctor and stated, "I am coming to prove that I am dead." He went on to explain that he did not need to eat or sleep, and his brain was already dead. The man, who suffered from depression and had previously attempted to take his own life, believed he had been successful in his attempt to electrocute himself in the bathtub months earlier. **When researchers took scans of the man's brain, they were surprised to find that parts of his brain had, in fact, shut down.**

In a chilling reminder of how little we really know about our brains, doctors were confounded by the man's scan results. As one of his doctors told *New Scientist*: "I've been analyzing PET scans for 15 years and I've never seen anyone who was on his feet, who was interacting with people, with such an abnormal scan result.... [His] brain function resembles that of someone during anaesthesia or sleep."

LIFE AFTER DEATH

According to *Healthline*, "Feeling like you've already died can lead to several complications." Those with Cotard's may starve themselves due to beliefs that they no longer need food, or attempt suicide in an endeavor to prove they can't "die again."

Cases of Cotard's syndrome are very rare, and each one is creepy in its own special way. In 2008, a New York woman begged her family members to bring her to the morgue so she could rest with the other dead—not only did she think she had died, but she believed she had begun to rot. In 2009, a Belgian man went to his doctor complaining he had died days ago but no one had taken it upon themselves to bury him. And in 1996, a Scottish man who had been in a motorcycle accident was convinced it had killed him. According to *Psychology Today*, he and his mother moved to South Africa, which further fed his delusions— apparently, only hell could be that hot.

RIP

STONE MAN SYNDROME

Also known as fibrodysplasia ossificans progressiva (FOP), stone man syndrome essentially means you're slowly becoming a statue: The incredibly rare disease causes your connective tissue—such as your tendons, muscles and ligaments—to turn into bone. This isn't great for your quality of life, as it causes difficulty of movement, eating, breathing and—well, that's pretty much the stuff that counts. *Most FOP patients are confined to their beds by age 20.*

Technically speaking, everyone's body is capable of turning cartilage into bone. It's how your bones grow larger as you become an adult, and normally, once you've reached your full size, this process stops. **But if you have FOP, bone growth doesn't stop—it just keeps growing abnormally, essentially creating a second skeleton over your connective tissue.** And once the bone grows, there isn't much doctors can do about it.

Ossification (bone-growing) is triggered whenever FOP patients have a minor injury. In one case, a London 12-year-old learned she had the disease after developing a hump on her back after falling down—the swollen area was slowly turning into bone, a terribly painful experience. By the time she turned 18, her neck and backbone had fused together, preventing her from lifting her arms above her waist.

NO SCRUBS

Surgery to remove excess bone growth is a no-go, as the procedure causes even more ossification.

TREE MAN SYNDROME

So-called for the bark-like growths that emerge from the body, tree man syndrome, or epidermodysplasia verruciformis, is a skin disorder that you should thank the lord you don't have. (**And if you do, we're very sorry.**)

The extraordinarily rare hereditary disorder causes wart-like lesions to appear all over your body. In time, **the warts morph and grow into long, bark-like tumors**. If it sounds incredibly unusual, that's because it is. As Dr. Michael Chernofsky said upon seeing a patient whose hands were covered in the tumors, "I've seen some weird things, but not this." To remove the painful warts and growths, the patient underwent surgery which left him with no skin on his hands—doctors replaced it with grafted skin from other parts of his body.

INCREDIBLE ODDS

While the disease comes from a strain of human papillomavirus (HPV), not everyone who has HPV is at risk of growing these tumors—you also need to have a genetic mutation that impedes your ability to handle the virus.

In another case, a Bangladeshi man had 24 operations to remove 11 pounds of growths from his hands and feet. Unfortunately, *removing the warts does not cure the disease*: A year later, the warts had returned.

ANEURYSM

Aneurysms happen when part of an artery wall becomes weak, causing it to widen abnormally or balloon out. It's especially not great when parts of your brain start swelling or, in worse cases, rupture. In about 40 percent of cases, ruptured brain aneurysms are fatal, and about two-thirds of survivors develop a permanent neurological deficit, according to the Brain Aneurysm Foundation.

If you do have an aneurysm, you might not have any idea unless it ruptures or expands quickly. (Though if the aneurysm occurs near the surface of your skin, you'll be able to tell by the painful swelling and visible throbbing mass, and should definitely get that checked out by a doctor.) **Sudden symptoms include pain, low blood pressure, shock, rapid heart rate, clammy skin, nausea, vomiting and dizziness**.

Though some factors like high blood pressure, high cholesterol and smoking can increase your risk of an aneurysm, doctors don't always know why they happen. Your best defense against them is living a healthy lifestyle and not being born with weak arteries.

IT'S ALL IN VEIN

Aneurysms don't only occur in your brain. Your heart, leg, intestines and spleen are all common places.

BLOOD CLOTS

Blood clotting is usually a good thing. As any hemophiliac can tell you, without the ability to clot, the most routine injury could cause you to bleed out. Once your wound heals, your body breaks down the clot and your life goes on as normal. But for some people, their blood may clot unnecessarily or clots won't dissolve properly. **And if a clot travels to your organs, you could be in for a very bad time.**

When a clot travels to your lungs and cuts off your blood flow, you have a pulmonary embolism. *If it travels to your heart, you have a stroke or heart attack.* Kidneys? Kidney failure. You get the picture.

You're more likely to have excessive blood clots if you're overweight, diabetic, have cancer, smoke or have a certain genetic disorder. They can also happen if you spend too much time in one position—*like if you're sitting on a plane...or reading a book about death for hours on end. Maybe take a second to stretch after you finish this entry?*

CELIAC DISEASE

Though celiac disease is more widely known thanks to the trendiness of eating gluten-free, it's a relatively rare condition—**only about 1 percent of people have the inherited autoimmune disease that makes eating gluten problematic.** For most people there's no upside to not eating gluten, despite what Gwyneth Paltrow says.

If you do have celiac disease, gluten can and will mess you up. *It causes an immune response in your intestines, damaging them over time.* This makes it impossible for your body to absorb certain nutrients, and also causes diarrhea, fatigue, anemia and weight loss.

Obviously not getting proper nutrition is bad—especially for growing kids. And once you're an adult, celiac disease can affect other parts of your body. Loss of bone density, itchy and blistery rashes, joint pain, mouth ulcers, and spleen and nervous system issues are all symptoms, so maybe don't roll your eyes the next time you see a gluten-free pizza—**it could save someone's life.**

EHLERS-DANLOS SYNDROME

Technically a group of 13 different disorders, Ehlers-Danlos syndrome (EDS) affects your connective tissues. *Depending on what kind of EDS you have, symptoms can range from being able to do some interesting party tricks to having life-threatening complications.*

People with EDS are usually even more bendy than a yoga instructor, thanks to defective collagen that makes their cartilage unusually weak. **While this sounds fun, it means their joints can be easily dislocated—a trait that is decidedly not fun.** Other annoying but mostly harmless side effects include fragile, stretchy skin, bruising like an extra-delicate peach and wounds that split open and get wider as they heal, leaving "cigarette paper" scars.

The most life-threatening form of the disorder is vascular EDS, which affects your blood vessels. If you're unlucky enough to be born with this disorder, your blood vessels could rupture unexpectedly, causing internal bleeding and a whole host of other issues. You're also more likely to have an organ rupture, and pregnancy is extremely dangerous—you're at a higher risk of intestine tears and uterine ruptures.

OFF WITH HER HEAD

In 2019, 52-year-old EDS patient Karen Pugh explained to *The Sun* that she wears a neck brace daily to help support her head; otherwise, her skull slips back and forth over the top of her spine. "I could decapitate myself. It's like [having] a watermelon balanced on a cocktail stick," she explained. "I'm at a daily risk of dying."

PICA

People with pica have been known to guzzle down all kinds of things that aren't normally considered food—*chalk, dirt, paint, pebbles, charcoal, paper, cloth, soap, string and ash* are all common non-food, non-nutritious items associated with the eating disorder.

Pica can be brought on by a few different reasons. **It can be a symptom of another mental health disorder, such as schizophrenia, or a sign of nutrient deficiency brought on by anemia, malnutrition or even pregnancy.** There are no lab tests for pica—generally, you or someone concerned for your well-being just tells your doctor you've been eating pebbles for at least the last month or so.

Obviously, there are a lot of potential issues that come with pica. Eating anything your body can't digest can cause an intestinal blockage, and you're really going against the "wash your food and hands" rule we've underlined throughout this book if you're eating dirt—at that point, you're begging for a parasitic infection.

RAPUNZEL SYNDROME

Similar to pica is Rapunzel syndrome, a disorder in which people compulsively eat their own hair. Also known as trichophagia, Rapunzel syndrome is also related to trichotillomania, a compulsion in which people pull out their own hair.

WORD OF THE DAY

A large mass of hair in your stomach is technically called a trichobezoar.

Eating hair on a regular basis can have dire consequences. In 2017, a 16-year-old girl in England died from the condition after the hairball in her stomach developed a "tail" that extended into her intestines. While this usually causes digestive problems, in the teen's case it also caused peritonitis (inflammation of the abdomen lining). This in turn can lead to inflammation throughout the body, making all of your organs shut down. *As previously mentioned, you need working organs to live.*

VAMPIRE SYNDROME

Clinically known as porphyria, vampire syndrome is a group of disorders caused by an excess of chemicals that produce porphyrin, an essential component in your blood. Too many porphyrins, however, could make people associate you with a certain count from Transylvania.

There are two types of porphyria—acute and cutaneous—and neither is particularly pleasant. Acute porphyria causes symptoms such as constipation, diarrhea, breathing problems, urination problems, red or brown urine, seizures, heart palpitations, muscle pain, paralysis and severe abdominal pain, among other symptoms. Acute porphyria can be severe if not properly treated.

Cutaneous porphyria is the type of the disease that may have caused people to think you were a vampire a few centuries ago. Sensitivity to the sun, fragile skin and red or brown urine are all both ancient signs of vampires as well as symptoms of cutaneous porphyria. *And though this version of the disease may cause you to get stabbed with a wooden stake, it's otherwise the lesser of two evils—sufferers of cutaneous porphyria mostly only need to worry about permanent skin damage.*

HEMOPHILIA

If you have hemophilia, a fairly rare disorder, your blood doesn't clot the way it should. On the bright side, you'll probably never die from a blood clot clogging your organs (page 201). But you do need to worry about getting injured, as you'll keep bleeding for much longer than most other people. *If your hemophilia is severe enough, you may even experience "spontaneous bleeding," according to the Mayo Clinic—and that's not the kind of spontaneity you should be highlighting on your dating profile.*

While you won't bleed out from a small cut, people with hemophilia are **at a serious risk of deep bleeding within their bodies**, especially in the knees, ankles and elbows. Joint damage is also a concern, as internal bleeding puts a lot of pressure on them.

THANKS, MOM

Most forms of hemophilia are inherited. The gene is passed via the X chromosome, meaning many women are carriers of the disease and are more likely to pass it on to any sons.

A bump on the head can also be life-threatening for those with severe hemophilia, as it could induce a brain bleed. Signs your brain is bleeding include an extremely painful headache that won't go away, feeling lethargic, continuous vomiting, seizures and double vision.

APOTEMNOPHILIA

If you're an apotemnophile, you have an incredibly intense and deep-rooted desire to amputate one of your limbs. Why you would want to do that is unclear—according to one paper, it may be a neurological disorder, connected to "congenital dysfunction of the right superior parietal lobule and its connection with the insula." Others suggest the disorder is psychiatric and may be a result of having seen an amputee at a young age.

The most Freudian (and probably wrong) suggested cause is that the remaining stump would have a phallic resemblance— somehow, that doesn't seem like enough motivation to hack off a part of your body.

> **BREAKING IT DOWN**
>
> In Greek, *apo* means "away from" and *temnien* means "to cut."

Since not many sane surgeons are willing to remove healthy limbs, determined apotemnophiles are known to take matters into their own hands (or hand, if they're getting rid of an arm) by severely damaging their own limb and forcing doctors to amputate. Ironically, those with the disorder often state they feel "complete" once the amputation has taken place.

In 2005, psychiatrist Michael First published what is probably still the largest study of apotemnophiles on record, with 52 subjects—14 of whom had successfully gotten an amputation. According to *Scientific American*, **"First uncovered people who'd crushed their legs under gym weights or used shotguns, chainsaws, a wood chipper and even dry ice to liberate an extraneous appendage."**

TRIMETHYLAMINURIA

Also known as "fish odor syndrome" or "stale fish syndrome," trimethylaminuria is a disorder with the charming side effect of making you smell as though you've been rolling around in fish that's been left out in the hot sun for a few days.

This happens because your body's metabolic process isn't working properly, causing trimethylamine, the same chemical that gives rotten fish its characteristically awful smell, to accumulate in your body. And if your body can't properly break down this chemical, that same smell will emanate from your breath, sweat and urine, meaning while you may not rack up as many dates, you'll probably always get a seat on the subway.

If you have fish odor syndrome, you can minimize your foul fumes by avoiding certain foods: Fish (obviously), eggs, liver, legumes and cruciferous vegetables like broccoli and cabbage all increase the amount of trimethylamine in your body. Other treatments include taking laxatives so food spends less time in your body or nutritional supplements such as activated charcoal or riboflavin to help decrease and break down the chemical.

LOVE STINKS

As one couple told the *Daily Mail*, having fish odor syndrome isn't necessarily a deal-breaker. Kelly Fidoe-White, who has the disorder, has been with her husband Michael for 16 years. As he said: "Kelly's smell has sometimes affected me in a negative manner but I haven't said anything to Kelly. I've just kept it to myself." And as Kelly points out about her husband, "he produces his own smell anyway."

LUPUS

Doctors don't always know why this autoimmune disease is brought on, but in many cases it's because a patient was born with a predisposition for this notorious disease that causes your body to attack itself. **Pretty much all of your body systems are at risk of becoming inflamed, including your skin, joints, blood cells, kidneys, brain, lungs and heart.**

FOLLOW THE BUTTERFLIES

The most clear sign of lupus is a butterfly-shaped rash across the face, but this doesn't appear in all cases of the disease.

If you are predisposed to lupus, flare-ups can be triggered by other infections, certain drugs or *simply being exposed to sunlight*. Flares, or episodes, include symptoms such as fatigue, joint pain, fever, skin lesions, shortness of breath, dry eyes, chest pain, headaches, confusion and memory loss. And as anyone who has ever seen *House* knows, the disease's symptoms overlap with many other ailments and there's no specific test for lupus, making it nearly impossible to diagnose.

Because it affects so many body systems, lupus is capable of causing further destruction all over your body. Strokes and seizures, bleeding in your lungs, heart attacks and kidney failure are all common and deadly complications of the disease. **Having lupus also puts you at a higher risk of contracting other life-threatening conditions, such as infections, pregnancy complications, cancer and bone tissue death.**

BRITTLE BONE DISEASE

Also known as osteogenesis imperfecta (OI), this genetic disorder causes people to be born with unusually frail bones that are easily broken. **Depending on the severity of the disorder, you could have just a handful or a few hundred bone fractures throughout your life.**

Tragically, the most severe form of OI is often fatal for newborns, as it causes extreme respiratory problems. In moderate cases, OI often causes people to be shorter than average, have a triangular face, brittle teeth, hearing loss, spinal curvature and mild to moderate bone deformity, on top of bones that are very likely to break, especially before puberty.

Treatment for brittle bone disease varies, but one of the more aggressive options is something called "rodding," which is eerily similar to the surgery that transformed superhero Logan, aka Wolverine, into Weapon X: *Surgeons insert metal rods along the length of the weak bones, which both strengthens them and can correct deformities.*

I WORK OUT

Unlike a lot of other bone disorders, people with OI are encouraged to exercise as much as possible, as it can increase bone and muscle strength, decreasing the likelihood of broken bones.

HUMAN-MADE MISERY

Staying super hydrated can kill you. Your reusable water bottle might carry a chemical that will help speed up the process. Feeling hungry? Microwave popcorn can literally take your breath away. And if reading this makes you want to take the edge off with a cigarette, definitely don't fall asleep. (Talk about getting lit.) Our mortality ensures that if nothing else kills us, we'll get the job done ourselves.

CIGARETTES

"The cure for the common cold." "For digestion's sake." "Give your throat a vacation." Old-school cigarette ads flew in the face of common sense to convince people smoking a cigarette was healthier than eating a salad, bad breath, yellowed teeth and hacking coughs be damned. Of course, the complete opposite is true, with regular tobacco use being tied to a laundry list of side effects ranging from **hearing loss, wrinkles and shortness of breath to fertility issues, impotence, emphysema, brain damage, heart disease and a variety of cancers**. *Give your body a vacation—from life!*

In 1964, the U.S. surgeon general confirmed that **cigarettes cause lung cancer**. You'd think that, even if the current population was too addicted to kick the habit, that would mean future generations would know better and not put cancer sticks in their mouths. Obviously, that's not what happened—at least, not right away. The tobacco industry suggested that experts disagreed about the evidence linking cigarettes to cancer, and *many people were happy to believe the companies they were buying cigarettes from instead of the surgeon general.*

Though the number of smokers in the U.S. has dramatically decreased— 14 percent of U.S. adults were smokers in 2017, compared to 42 percent in 1964—**smoking is still the leading cause of preventable death in the world**. According to the CDC, tobacco causes more than 7 million deaths each year worldwide, and more than 480,000 deaths each year in the U.S.

Cigarettes also pose an obvious threat to the human body that humans could never claim ignorance of: fire. In 1951, a woman named Mary Reeser was suspected to have died of spontaneous human combustion. What little was left of her had been found in her apartment, along with a scorched rug. Surrounding plastic objects had melted and lost their shape, but other than that, there were no signs of fire in the apartment. Authorities eventually declared that Reeser, who was known to take sleeping pills, must have fallen unconscious while smoking a cigarette, setting fire to her acetate nightgown and housecoat.

BPAs

Short for bisphenol A, BPA is a chemical that has been standard in certains kinds of plastics and resins since the 1960s. Though it was first discovered in the 1890s, humans didn't get the bright idea to use it in food products until about 60 years later, when we realized it helped create tough plastics.

BONUS BPAs

BPAs aren't only found in plastics. The chemical is also commonly used in canned foods, toiletries, feminine hygiene products, dental filling sealants and sports equipment, among other things.

Unfortunately, it probably wasn't a good idea to use BPAs in plastics that store food or in resins that line cans—though as of 2014 the FDA says the amount of BPA that occurs in food is safe, there is a fair amount of research to the contrary. Higher levels of BPAs have been linked to obesity, heart disease, type 2 diabetes and infertility in both men and women.

Pregnant women in particular should be aware of the risks of BPAs. Some research has shown the chemical can adversely affect the brains and prostate glands of fetuses. **And according to one study, children born to mothers who had higher BPA levels were more depressed, anxious and hyperactive.** Because of research like this, use of BPAs has been restricted in Canada, China, Malaysia and the EU, especially in products for babies and toddlers.

ANTIBIOTIC RESISTANCE

Though antibiotics were very much a miracle drug—the number of deaths from ailments like pneumonia have nosedived since their discovery, and anyone who's ever had a UTI will certainly sing their praises—*overuse of antibiotics has really bit the human race in the ass.*

Because bacteria are capable of becoming antibiotic-resistant, it is becoming increasingly difficult to treat many bacterial infections such as blood poisoning, gonorrhea and tuberculosis. While this was somewhat of an inevitable outcome, humans have streamlined the process for bacteria to become resistant by over-prescribing antibiotics, not following directions to finish treatments and using leftover antibiotics to treat other infections.

IF I COULD TURN BACK TIME

According to the World Health Organization, lack of action on how we use antibiotics means we are "heading for a post-antibiotic era, in which common infections and minor injuries can once again kill." To recall what that's like, see Plague on page 154.

There are a few things you can do to help keep bacteria from becoming completely resistant to anything humans can throw against it. These include mostly obvious steps like only taking antibiotics prescribed by your doctor, following the instructions for taking them and preventing infections in the first place by getting vaccinated as necessary, washing your hands and food and practicing safe sex.

MICROWAVE POPCORN

In 2007, major popcorn manufacturers removed the chemical that had been linked to a serious lung disease you can get from—wait for it—huffing microwave popcorn: **popcorn lung**, which is easily one of the weirdest ways you can ruin your lungs.

Though this sounds like something that would only happen in an off-brand version of Candy Land, it's very real and very scary, thanks to the chemical diacetyl, which is used to give kernels a buttery flavor and aroma. *(Note: You can also get a buttery flavor and aroma from butter.)* Sufferers of popcorn lung (aka bronchiolitis obliterans) have scarred and narrowed bronchioles (airways), which makes it difficult to let in enough air. Like COPD (page 175), the disease causes wheezing and shortness of breath, among other respiratory issues.

All of that being said, it takes a lot of diacetyl to cause popcorn lung—most of those affected worked in microwave popcorn factories. However, you can still get popcorn lung if you eat enough microwave popcorn from a brand that hasn't removed diacetyl. In 2012, one Colorado man with the disease sued Gilster-Mary Lee Corp, which manufactured the bags of popcorn he had been consuming twice a day for 10 years. As his doctor testified: "We cannot be sure that this patient's exposure to butter-flavored microwave popcorn from daily heavy preparation has caused his lung disease. However, we have no other plausible explanation."

EATING YOURSELF TO DEATH

Obesity is linked to a whole range of health issues, and too much sugar, processed meat and fried foods will all probably shorten your lifespan. **But it's also possible to eat so much in one sitting that you quite literally rupture your stomach.**

Your body doesn't want to let you eat so much you explode—usually you'll vomit long before you reach that point. But people with eating disorders or who have trained themselves to push past the nausea (think competitive eaters) are more likely to reach that breaking point.

According to Dr. Rachel Vreeman, assistant professor of pediatrics at Indiana University School of Medicine: "Their bodies' reflexes have been ignored or abused for so long that they no longer vomit at the appropriate time. And then once the stomach gets to this extremely distended point, the stomach muscles are too stretched out to be strong enough to vomit the food out." If you eat enough food, your stomach's walls will weaken and tear, spilling food and bile into other parts of your abdomen. Not only is this incredibly painful, it will definitely turn your blood septic and you'll need surgery to save your life.

LET HIM EAT CAKE

In 1771, Swedish King Adolf Frederick died of "digestive problems" after eating a Shrove Tuesday meal of champagne, lobster, kippers, caviar, boiled meats, sauerkraut and turnips, followed by 14 semlas (sweet buns) served in hot milk with cinnamon and raisins.

Human-Made Misery

rBGH

In an effort to get as much dairy as possible out of our cows, Americans inject them with a hormone that increases milk production. And while there are no regulations on recombinant bovine growth hormone (rBGH) in the United States, it has been banned in the European Union, Australia and Canada—apparently, the U.S. values extra gallons of milk over possibly increasing the risk of cancer.

While we can't say for sure that rBGH causes cancer, we do know that it increases cow milk production by increasing levels of a hormone known as IGF-1. **We also know that increased levels of IGF-1 in humans has been linked to multiple kinds of breast, colon, prostate and other cancers, so it's not looking great.**

WHAT'S THE PUS?

Compared to untreated milk, rBST milk also has increased somatic cell counts, or pus. According to a 2010 court decision regarding milk labels, more pus "[makes] the milk turn sour more quickly and is another indicator of poor milk quality."

Since its approval by the FDA in 1993, the U.S. has used rBGH without any regulations. *However, American consumers who want to enjoy a glass of milk or slice of cheese without worrying about carcinogens are being heard, as multiple large chains such as Publix, Kroger and Chipotle reduce or eliminate rBGH products in their stores.*

WATER INTOXICATION

Water makes up about 66 percent of your body, and every one of your cells needs it. But it's very possible to get too much—many people have killed themselves by chugging water.

If you over-hydrate, you could wind up with a condition called hyponatremia, a word with Latin and Greek roots that roughly translates to "insufficient salt in the blood." In other words, you're literally diluting your blood as your kidneys can't flush the water out fast enough. Excess water then enters your cells: This is particularly bad in your brain cells, which aren't built to expand. *Once you've reached the brain-swelling stage, you can expect seizures, coma, respiratory arrest, brain stem herniation and death.*

HEATING A LAVA LAMP

In 2004, a 24-year-old man in Washington named Philip Quinn had the totally groovy (and completely idiotic) idea to put a lava lamp on his hot stove. We'll never know what sparked the decision—perhaps it was a desire to make the blobs move faster, curiosity or a simple mistake. As local police spokesperson Paul Peterson said, "Why on earth he was heating a lava lamp on the stove, we don't know."

What we do know is that it was a terrible choice that led to a freak accident. **Heating the lava lamp on the stove caused it to explode, sending pieces of glass into Quinn's chest, including one fatal shard that entered his heart.**

ANTI-VAXXERS

Despite the fact that there is absolutely no link between vaccines and autism—the 1998 study by British surgeon Andrew Wakefield that initially made the correlation was discredited for many reasons, and multiple further studies found no evidence to support the idea—some people, *most of whom do not have a medical or scientific degree*, insist the connection is there. For example, actor and comedian Rob Schneider, aka Deuce Bigalow: Male Gigolo, has been outspoken against vaccines, stating, "We're having more and more autism," in a 2012 interview.

Whether people incorrectly believe vaccines cause autism or are railing against the government's ability to enforce medical procedures, the result is the same— **refusing to vaccinate children is jeopardizing our "herd immunity**," which only exists as long as enough of the population is vaccinated, preventing infectious diseases from spreading.

Not only do vaccines protect the individual, they protect those who cannot get them, including infants, pregnant women, the elderly and those with compromised immune systems. Americans are already seeing the effects of lower rates of vaccination. In 2010, there were 9,120 cases of whooping cough in California, more than there have been since the whooping cough vaccine began being offered in the 1940s. During the outbreak, 10 infants too young to be vaccinated died from the disease.

IF YOU AIN'T TAKING SHOTS...

Other famous figures who have questioned vaccines include Kirstie Alley, Selma Blair, Jim Carrey, Cindy Crawford, Robert De Niro, Jenny McCarthy, Charlie Sheen, Alicia Silverstone and Donald Trump.

PESTICIDES

To be fair, pesticides do a lot of good—**without them, more than half of the world's crops would be inedible due to diseases and pests.** But overreliance on pesticides can be dangerous, as too much exposure to pesticides can lead to serious health problems.

If you find yourself on the wrong end of a pesticide sprayer without a mask, *you'd experience symptoms such as eye and skin irritation, respiratory tract infection, nausea, vomiting, diarrhea and headache.* If you breathe in enough, you could also lose consciousness, start seizing or die.

Long-term exposure to lower levels of pesticides have been linked to asthma, depression, anxiety, Parkinson's disease, ADHD and certain kinds of cancer. To limit your exposure to pesticides, the EPA suggests rinsing your produce under running water and keeping pests out of your home by keeping it clean—crumbs and puddles are roach magnets—instead of dousing it with chemicals.

STORM DRAINS

Storm drains can be deadly, even without murderous clowns named Pennywise hiding within them. These unsuspecting holes in the ground are lurking on every suburban street, just waiting for someone to be foolish enough to climb into one.

There have been at least two storm drain-related deaths in recent memory. In 2018, a woman named Rebecca Bunting descended into a sewer in Philadelphia with her boyfriend to take photos. The arrival of a flash flood caused water to rush through the sewer, sweeping Bunting away around 6 p.m. Her body was found at 10:45 a.m. the next morning.

In 2008, a 57-year-old man in Canada died after attempting to retrieve his wallet from a storm drain. When he was unable to reach it, he removed the grate, crawled in and got stuck—a police officer found him wedged in the street but still alive, and a tow truck was needed to pull him out. Unfortunately, the man died at the hospital shortly after.

RED AND PROCESSED MEATS

In what felt like a targeted attack on the average American diet, the International Agency for Research on Cancer announced in 2015 it was classifying processed meat as a carcinogen and red meat as a probable carcinogen. *In other words, eating too many hot dogs and hamburgers is increasing our risk of cancer—especially if you top them with bacon.*

The connection between meat and bowel cancer has been traced to three things: **haem, a red pigment found in red meat; nitrates and nitrites, which are used to keep processed meat fresh; and heterocyclic amines and polycyclic amines, which are produced when meat is cooked at high temperatures.** In other words, eating a freshly grilled sausage is the ideal way to damage the cells in your bowels.

Experts found eating about 2 ounces of processed meats (anything that has been salted, cured, fermented or smoked, such as sausages, ham and some deli meats) per day *increased the risk of colorectal cancer by 18 percent*. And red meat, such as beef, pork, lamb and goat, has been linked to colorectal, pancreatic and prostate cancer.

WHERE'S THE BEEF?

Commonsense ways to reduce cancer-causing meat intake include replacing half your meat with beans or lentils, eating vegetarian on some days and choosing chicken, fish or a plant-based meat alternative instead.

VENDING MACHINES

According to a 1992 study, at least 64 people have been injured by tipping vending machines, with 15 of the injuries being deadly. The victims were men in all but one case, most of them young—the average age of the victims was 19.8 years. *(We're betting studies like these have something to do with high rates of car insurance for male teens.)*

I'VE GOT A CRUSH ON YOU

According to *The Guardian*, two people in the U.S. die from falling vending machines each year.

The author of the study, Michael Q. Cosio, had published an earlier paper on the subject in 1988. In that study, he examined 15 cases, three of which were fatal. The injuries ranged from fractured skulls and a partial toe amputation to a punctured bladder and multiple bone and ligament injuries.

The fatal cases were particularly gruesome. One man was found by his wife and "took four men to lift the soda machine off the victim," another was "found pinned to a wall with the soda machine resting on his neck" and the last one was crushed when his friend "could no longer hold up the machine." So as tempting as it is to shake the machine to get the undelivered soda you paid for, maybe walk to the janitor's office instead. *It's better than a trip to the hospital—or the morgue.*

FRUIT JUICE INJECTION

While fruit juice is not the healthiest choice, as juicing strips a fruit of its fiber and water-soluble nutrients, it's also far from the worst thing you can put in your body. Unless, of course, your idea of having a glass of fruit juice involves a needle.

In 2019, one Chinese woman answered the question no one was asking—**"Can you juice with actual juice?"**—by making her own juice from 20 different fruits and then intravenously injecting the liquid. As it turns out, the answer is no: *The 51-year-old gave herself itchy skin and an increased temperature, and wound up damaging her liver, kidney, heart and lungs.* Her treatment required five days in intensive care, dialysis and antibiotics, meaning she likely would have died without immediate care.

According to the woman, who survived the incident, "I had thought fresh fruits were very nutritious and it would not do me harm by injecting them into my body." **Clearly, she was wrong.**

DIET SUPPLEMENTS

People who are looking to take a shortcut in losing weight risk a lot more than disappointment if they turn to unregulated diet pills for help—especially if the pills contain DNP, aka 2,4-dinitrophenol, an industrial chemical normally used as a pesticide.

The pills, which are often marketed as "fat-burning" supplements, are easy enough to find online. *And though they do burn fat, they also cause your body to overheat, which can cause side effects that vary from nausea and vomiting to irregular heartbeat and coma, or even death.*

The pills have been particularly problematic in the U.K., where DNP poisoning rates have sharply increased—there were only three cases between 2007 and 2011. Since 2012, however, there have been at least 115 cases reported.

MARGARINE

In the 1970s, public health authorities recommended that Americans limit their intake of butter, as it was high in saturated fats, which recent studies had linked to heart disease. Unable to tolerate the idea of not slathering pancakes, popcorn or potatoes with something that at least resembled butter, *people turned to margarine, its vegetable oil-based, we-can-definitely-believe-it's-not-butter doppelgänger.*

Unfortunately, people didn't realize margarine was even worse for you than butter. Thanks to the process used to harden vegetable oils, margarine was high in trans fats and therefore much worse for your heart— trans fats both raise your bad cholesterol and lower your good cholesterol. And while it's recommended that you limit your saturated fats, you should avoid trans fats altogether.

Today, many margarine manufacturers have switched to a process that doesn't add trans fats, but that shouldn't be considered a free pass to put a few tablespoons on a bagel every morning—the spread is still high in calories.

CLIMATE CHANGE

While climate change is a complex topic, it boils down to this: **Carbon dioxide and other greenhouse gases make our atmosphere hotter by trapping heat**. *And by burning fossil fuels such as oil, natural gas and coal, humans are releasing incredible amounts of carbon pollution, trapping ever-increasing amounts of heat in the air.*

The effects of our hotter atmosphere—**it has increased 2 degrees F over the last century**—are easily observable. For example, because climate change increases the likelihood of heavy rainfall, it increases the risk of floods (page 109). And the number of deaths due to floods is on the rise. In the last 30 years, an average of 86 people died in floods each year. In the last decade, that average rose to 95, and since 2015, more than 100 people have died because of flooding each year.

According to NASA, other effects of climate change we've already seen and should expect to worsen include **loss of sea ice, rising sea levels, stronger hurricanes, longer and hotter heat waves, and more droughts**.

FACT OR LOBBYIST

Though the fossil fuel industry would like you to believe the science on climate change is debatable, it is decidedly not. Ninety-seven percent of climate scientists agree humans are contributing to climate change.

MAN-MADE FLOODS

While natural floods are caused by heavy rain and rising tides, man-made floods are caused by neglect or idiocy. Things like burst water heaters, backed-up sewer systems and broken pipes can flood your home, and all count as man-made floods. However, while these small examples usually don't kill anyone, massive man-made floods—*like the 1814 beer flood in London or the 1919 molasses flood in Boston*—certainly do.

In 1814, more than 100,000 gallons of beer broke free from a vat, creating a 15-foot-high wave of porter that crashed through the streets of London. As one witness recounted, "All at once, I found myself borne onward with great velocity by a torrent which burst upon me so suddenly, as almost to deprive me of breath." While he was lucky enough to be rescued from the deluge, others weren't—and their families probably weren't pleased that jurors declared the incident an "unavoidable act of God" instead of blaming the company for faulty vats, as the decision meant those who lost their loved ones or houses received no recompense.

Just more than 100 years later, a similar event occurred in Boston when *more than 2 million gallons of molasses broke free from flawed steel tanks*—before the incident, children used to bring cups to the tank and catch molasses from the tanks' cracks. **The sticky substance ran down the streets at up to 35 miles per hour, killing 21 people and injuring 150 more.** Apparently, you could still smell the molasses decades later.

COAL EMISSIONS

Using coal as a power source is problematic for two reasons. For one, it contributes to the greenhouse gases heating up our environment (see Climate Change on page 226). But even putting that awful side effect aside, coal does direct damage to people who breathe it in. There's a reason no one wants to get coal from Santa on Christmas—it's dirty, and working with coal or inhaling its fumes is not advised for your health.

On top of adding carbon to our air, coal is responsible for 42 percent of U.S. mercury emissions (see more about mercury on page 230). In 2014, U.S. coal plants also released 3.1 million tons of sulfur dioxide and 1.5 million tons of nitrogen oxides in the air, plus almost 200,000 tons of soot. *Combined, these toxic chemicals are linked to asthma, chronic bronchitis, pneumonia, influenza, heart attacks and premature death, plus ecological side effects such as smog and acid rain.*

BUT WAIT, THERE'S MORE

In 2014, the U.S. coal industry was also responsible for 576,185 tons of carbon monoxide, 22,124 tons of volatile organic compounds, 77,108 pounds of arsenic, 41.2 tons of lead, 9,332 pounds of cadmium and other toxic heavy metals, none of which are good for the environment or your lungs.

DIESEL ENGINE EXHAUST

According to OSHA *(and everyone with a smidge of common sense)*, **it is not wise to inhale a lot of diesel engine exhaust**. But if you're a miner, construction worker, truck driver, farm worker or mechanic, you might not have a lot of choice in the matter.

When diesel fuel combusts in an engine, it does a lot more than make the machine go. It also releases two different kinds of carbon into the air, one which includes something called polyaromatic hydrocarbons (PAH). *Again, carbon is very bad for the environment (see Climate Change on page 226), but it's also very bad for your body.*

In their 2013 hazard alert regarding diesel exhaust, OSHA cautions that some PAHs caused cancer when tested in animals. They also advise exposure to diesel exhaust increases risk of eye and nose irritation, headaches, nausea, lung cancer and respiratory disease.

SHOOTING A PROTECTED CACTUS

While most humans are contributing to the demise of the Earth and our own existence through small actions, some really go right for the source. *This was the case with David Grundman, who in 1982 decided to have some fun with his roommate James Suchochi by shooting at protected cacti in the Arizona desert.*

The two first felled a smaller saguaro cactus by pumping it full of bullets before moving on to a larger, older saguaro, estimated to be 26 feet tall and about a century old. After shooting at its 4-foot, spike-covered arm, Grundman decided to poke at it to help it fall off. **It worked too well, as the 500-pound arm promptly fell from the tree and onto Grundman, crushing and killing him.**

TIME TO FACE THE MUSIC

Grundman's death is forever immortalized in the song "Saguaro" by Texas's own Austin Lounge Lizards.

MERCURY POISONING

You've probably heard the phrase "mad as a hatter," which is a colorful way of describing someone whose mental health is not doing all that well. The etymology of the phrase is most likely quite literal: In the 1700s and 1800s, workers using mercury nitrate to turn fur into felt for hats developed a range of mental and physical issues, **including speech problems, tremors, hallucinations and emotional instability.** *In other words, the hatters were going mad.*

The problem was particularly prevalent in Danbury, Connecticut, which was the site of many hatmakers until the early-20th century. In fact, residents of the state called the poisoning's trademark tremors "Danbury shakes." In other areas, the tremors were also called "hatter's shakes."

It's highly unlikely to get mercury poisoning in most developed countries today; France and England stopped using mercury around 1900, and its use was outlawed in the U.S. in 1941. But mercury poisoning still occurs in developing countries, where it's used to extract gold from mined rocks. **Sadly, there's no treatment for mercury poisoning— the damage it does is permanent.**

MAD AS A GILDER

In the popular 2017 podcast *S-Town*, it's suggested that subject John McLemore may have been affected by mercury poisoning. McLemore regularly used mercury as part of fire gilding, a technique he favored for adding embellishments to his restored antique clocks.

MUSLIN DISEASE

In the late-1700s and early-1800s, many Parisian women favored the fashion trend of dampening their bodies before dressing in their muslin gowns, which made the fabric cling more closely to their figures. *This sounds wildly risqué for the time period, but then again, we are talking about France.*

Apparently, the style came about after the Sumptuary Laws decreed women in lower classes could not wear clothes and accessories totaling more than 3.5 kilograms in weight, *as heavier fabrics were to be reserved for the upper class.* In strict adherence with the law, many women chose not to wear underwear, further exposing themselves in the wet muslin.

Unfortunately, the women's attempts at malicious compliance backfired, as wetting down the little clothing you're wearing in cold temperatures is a great way to increase your chances of catching pneumonia. **At the time, some hygienists also blamed the trend for Paris's influenza outbreak in 1803, labeling the sickness "muslin disease."**

CHUBBY BUNNY

In what's supposed to be a fun game, Chubby Bunny involves saying a chosen phrase (such as "chubby bunny") as you fill your mouth with marshmallows. The more full your mouth is, the more your cheeks puff out like a bunny's and the harder it is to say the phrase. Whoever can fit the most marshmallows in their mouth while enunciating the words is the winner. *However, you should probably play a game that isn't also a choking hazard.*

In 1999, a 12-year-old choked on just four marshmallows while playing the game at her elementary school's annual Care Fair, and tragically passed at the hospital a few hours later. In 2006, a 32-year-old woman suffered the same fate while playing the game in Ontario. The game is so perilous because of the nature of marshmallows—their consistency makes them difficult to extract by Heimlich maneuver or medical instruments if one gets lodged in the throat.

SELFIES

For some unknowable reason, the advent of the smartphone has compelled countless people to take photos of themselves in increasingly dangerous places "for the 'Gram." Putting oneself in a dangerous position in pursuit of likes already increases the risk of death—after all, whether you're perched on the edge of a cliff or have just climbed over the guardrail at a zoo, your chances of getting maimed or killed increase. But leaning back to get the lighting and angle just right while also dedicating one of your hands to taking that perfect snap (instead of holding a railing or fending off a grizzly) changes the equation even further, and not in a good way.

> ### FLASHING LIGHTS
>
> In July 2015, an English hiker was killed when a sudden thunderstorm turned his metal selfie stick into a lightning rod.

In the worst cases, taking photos of your own bad judgment can also kill the people around you. **According to *The New York Times*, a selfie may have been partly to blame in a fatal helicopter crash over Manhattan in March 2018.** The pilot of the helicopter (the only survivor of the incident) suspects a passenger who was trying to photograph his feet hanging out of the open helicopter door may have accidentally hit the emergency fuel shut-off, causing the crash that killed him and the other four passengers.

TANNING BED

Most people understand that getting a sunburn is not good for your skin (the pain is a bit of a giveaway), but it's not as obvious that tanning is bad for you too. Whether the UV rays burn your skin or, well, tan it, they're still terrible for you. **Not only does tanning lead to premature wrinkles and leathery skin, it also increases your risk of skin cancer.**

While dermatologists are begging people to wear protective clothing, slather themselves in SPF 30 and stay in the shade as much as possible, *around 35 percent of American adults do the opposite by stripping down and crawling into boxes that give off cancer-causing UV rays*. This is not good: Using a tanning bed before you turn 35 can increase your risk of melanoma, the deadliest form of skin cancer, by up to 59 percent. The odds get worse whenever you work on your tan.

NEED FOR UVs

In a 2017 study done by Georgetown University Medical Center, 20 percent of women who tanned showed signs of "tanning dependency."

TRIPPING ON YOUR OWN BEARD

In the 1560s, an Austrian man named Hans Steininger made the questionable decision of growing his beard out as long as possible, resulting in *facial hair that reached the impressive length of 4.5 feet*. He is remembered as having the lengthiest chin hairs in history. Unfortunately, his achievement was also his downfall.

As the story goes, Steininger usually kept his beard rolled up in a leather pouch to keep it from interfering in his other, non-beard-growing activities, but had neglected to do so on a fateful day in 1567 when a fire broke out. In his rush to escape, **Steininger tripped over his own beard and fell down a flight of stairs, breaking his neck.**

If you want to see Steininger's beard for yourself, you can—more than 450 years later, it's still on display in a museum in Braunau am Inn, his hometown.

ASBESTOS

According to a vintage advertisement, asbestos is the "**magic mineral of the Middle Ages**." To be fair, this naturally occurring fiber has a lot of great qualities—once separated into fibers, it's surprisingly fluffy, not to mention naturally resistant to electricity, fire and corrosion. It also makes for effective insulation and can be used to strengthen materials such as paper, cloth, plastic and cement. *Then again, there's that tiny issue of asbestos being highly toxic— humans should have known this "magic mineral" was too good to be true.*

Asbestos has been used in North America since the late-1800s and became very popular during World War II. For decades, it could be found in everything from insulation and roofing to tiles and paints in buildings to vehicle brake pads in cars—**and even certain kinds of crayons**.

FREEDOM FIBERS

Asbestos is illegal in many countries, but has not yet been banned in the U.S.

The fibers are most dangerous when they are "friable," or easily crumbled, which releases the fibers into the air where they can be inhaled by humans. *Once the fibers are in your body, they can't be broken down or removed*, and will eventually cause disease. Asbestosis (scarred lung tissue), lung cancer and mesothelioma are all commonly caused by asbestos inhalation.

In 2019, a retired professor from Metro State University in Denver informed local reporters that the West Classroom in which she worked had a history of asbestos and had been nicknamed the "cancer corner." As she told the local ABC affiliate: "Colon cancer, skin cancer, sarcoma in a neck. We have bladder cancer, two breast cancers. Out of 14 people, we had 10 different people diagnosed with a variety of cancers." While those seem like damning odds, the university has refrained from closing the building until tests prove that 71 percent of its workers getting cancer isn't just an incredible, terrible coincidence.

VIDEO GAME ADDICTION

Playing tons of video games generally isn't good for your health—unless you're an especially enthusiastic *Mario Party* player or you're still hooked on *Dance Dance Revolution*—as being stationary for hours on end every day increases your risk of both cardiovascular disease and cancer.

But while most people who game are slowly dooming themselves, **there are examples of people who literally played until they ran out of their own life**. In 2015, a 32-year-old in Taiwan was found dead in an internet café after playing for three days straight—he was rushed to a hospital after employees found him slumped over a table, and pronounced dead from cardiac failure. Even more disturbing, however, was the reaction of other gamers in the cafe—*according to CNN, police said they "continued as if nothing happened even when the police and paramedics arrived."*

GAME OVER

In 2012, a 23-year-old man's corpse sat for 13 hours in a New Taipei City internet café before staff and other gamers realized he'd died.

This wasn't the first time a gamer had died in one of Taiwan's internet cafés—*a week earlier a 38-year-old man had been found dead after playing games for five days straight.*

POKÉMON GO

In 2016, people all over the world stopped paying attention to actual reality and got lost in the augmented reality of *Pokémon Go*, **the app that superimposes the often-adorable "pocket monsters" onto your surroundings.** This sometimes had dire consequences, especially when people paid more attention to their smartphone than their steering wheels, children or any cliffs along their path.

According to some estimates, *Pokémon Go* may have been responsible for *150,000 traffic accidents and 256 deaths in its first 148 days,* thanks to its ability to make users behave as if they've been hit with Confusion attacks.

Among the most outrageous examples (aside from distracted driving) included an Arizona couple who were arrested for leaving their toddler outside in 90-degree heat while they searched for Zubats for at least an hour and a half; the man who walked straight off a cliff and fell 75 to 100 feet, requiring firefighters to rescue him (and the other unconscious man who had done the same thing earlier); and a woman who needed to call firefighters to help her down from a tree that she had climbed while playing the game.

GOTTA CATCH 'EM ALL

Wanted criminal William Wilcox was recognized and apprehended after he walked straight into a Michigan police station, which was listed as a *Pokémon Go* "gym."

ALCOHOL

While moderate amounts of alcohol can potentially be good for you—**it may be associated with lower risks of stroke, heart attack and diabetes**—people who drink regularly tend to push far past what doctors mean when they say "moderate." To be clear, that's up to two drinks per day for men and, thanks to differences in enzymes, one drink or less per day for women *(and no, "saving" your drinks to use on the weekend doesn't count)*.

Over long periods of time, *regular excessive drinking ravages pretty much every part of your body.* Colon, breast and liver cancer, liver disease, higher risks of dementia, high blood pressure and heart failure are common consequences of hitting the bottle too hard, not to mention the potential for drunk driving, dangerous falls and other risky behaviors.

Of course, it's also possible to literally drink yourself to death in one sitting. About 2,200 Americans die this way each year—fatalities are most common in people between 35 and 64 years old.

COCAINE

Cocaine is a wildly powerful and addictive drug made from the leaves of South America's coca plant. And while it's sometimes used as a local anesthetic, snorting, smoking or injecting cocaine is pretty much guaranteed to mess you up.

The fair-to-positive side effects of cocaine are enlarged pupils, increased energy and euphoria. *The negative side effects include erratic and violent behavior, insomnia, psychosis, heart attack, seizure, coma and, in many cases, a sudden urge to poop.* Long-term effects include loss of sense of smell, infection and death of bowel tissue and lung damage. But thanks to cocaine's ability to literally alter your brain's chemistry, your body and mind will rely on the drug, making overdose and death all the more likely.

HELL'S KITCHEN

After losing a close friend to cocaine in 2003, Gordon Ramsay decided to make a documentary on the drug. In what became a viral video from the film, Ramsay watches a man in Colombia chop coca leaves, then add cement, sulphuric acid, gas and battery acid before separating the clear cocaine water from the mixture.

PLASTIC CAPS

If you're the kind of person who likes to chew on pen caps (or anything else not meant to be chewed on), you should probably rethink that habit. *Choking on a cap can happen to anyone,* from the 13-year-old boy who died in 2007 to famed playwright Tennessee Williams, who was found in his New York hotel room with a bottle cap in his throat.

Pen manufacturers have even tried to prevent deaths by making caps with vented tops, decreasing the chance of suffocation if the cap becomes lodged in someone's throat. **Still, around 100 people in the U.S. die each year from pen caps, though apparently that figure used to be higher.**

OPIOIDS

Humans just can't seem to quit opioids, a class of drugs that includes classics such as heroin, fentanyl, oxycodone, codeine and morphine. Though for a while it seemed like their heyday had passed—you don't see bottles of laudanum at the pharmacy anymore—opioid overdose fatalities are on the rise, especially in places like Minnesota. *According to the Minnesota Department of Human Services, deaths from opioid overdose have increased 430 percent since 2000.*

Despite what your D.A.R.E. officer may have told you, prescription painkillers are much more likely than weed to be the "gateway drug" to heroin. As the CDC states, opioid painkiller prescriptions quadrupled between 1999 and 2015—in other words, doctors were handing them out like candy. **And because opioids are highly addictive, people started turning to heroin when their doctors finally cut them off.**

REVERSE, REVERSE

Opioid overdoses can be reversed if the drug naloxone is given immediately. Many states have programs that offer free doses of naloxone as well as training for administering it.

If you take a large dose of opioids, there's a significant risk of overdosing (which usually includes pinpoint pupils, respiratory depression and death). The risk gets higher when you combine opioids with alcohol and sedatives.

LEAD

According to the World Health Organization, there are no known safe levels of lead exposure. This is bad news for humans, *as we've put lead in jewelry, paint, stained glass, ceramic glazes and cosmetics, not to mention gasoline and aviation fuel.*

Disturbingly, lead can also be ingested by drinking water delivered via lead pipes, or by using some traditional medicines. Lead does serious damage to your body, increasing risks of high blood pressure, stroke and cardiovascular disease.

If you thought lead-related deaths went down after we stopped putting it in paint, you'd be wrong—a 2018 study found that more than 400,000 deaths each year in the U.S. are caused by lead, a figure 10 times higher than researchers previously thought.

THE KIDS ARE NOT ALRIGHT

Not only are young children more likely to ingest lead-based things, they absorb four to five times as much ingested lead as adults do.

PLANKING

Planking (aka having someone take a photo of you lying stiff as a board, face-down in an unexpected place) took the internet by storm in 2011. While it was common to see photos of people planking on park benches, office desks or laundry machines, some took the fad to the next level by planking in more precarious places, such as railroad tracks, smoke stacks or on industrial machinery.

In September of that year, one Wisconsin teen was cited $202.20 for planking on a parked police car. Capt. Scott Luchterhand, who issued the disorderly conduct citation, later stated it "goes without saying" that police officers don't want people doing that.

Unfortunately, citations were not the worst outcome for some plankers. One Australian man in New South Wales was in an induced coma after falling from the roof of a moving car; another Australian in Brisbane died after falling off a seventh-floor balcony.

YELLOWSTONE HOT SPRINGS

Famous for its geysers and hot springs, **Yellowstone National Park is one of the more hazardous natural attractions in the United States**. Though you're in very little danger if you heed the warnings (apparently there's always a small risk of being hit by a falling tree), more than 20 people have directly caused their own death by ignoring warning signs and trying to take a dip in the hot springs, which can reach boiling temperatures.

TOXIC TOOTS

Toxic gases may accumulate in the park's hydrothermal areas, so the National Park Service advises leaving the geyser basins immediately if you begin to feel sick.

In a horrifying incident from 2016, an Oregon man and his sister illegally left the park's boardwalk to check the temperature of the acidic, boiling waters of the Norris Geyser basin. The man fell into the 10-foot deep pool, leading to his death.

According to Park Ranger Phil Strehle's account of the accident, officials judged the man to be dead from afar based on his burns and lack of movement. They were unable to recover his body that evening due to nightfall and lightning storms; **by the next day, his body had dissolved**, leaving behind his wallet and melted flip-flops.

TIDE PODS

In 2017, **teens once again proved their propensity for doing stupid things** with the "Tide Pod Challenge," in which you're supposed to let the brand-name laundry detergent pods dissolve in your mouth. Despite the fact that there had been a fair amount of media coverage touting the dangers of storing detergent where a toddler could accidentally eat it, some teens seemed to think they'd be just fine.

To keep children from eating Tide Pods, Tide began coating them with something called Bitrex in 2015. The bitter substance makes you feel nauseous and causes vomiting. If you push past this, the cleaning agents will burn your mouth and cause it to swell. Actually swallowing a pod can cause your windpipe to shrink, leaving you needing a ventilator to breathe. *Swallowing multiple pods would yield bloody vomit, ulcers, blood loss in the digestive tract, bubbly saliva and death.*

RUNNING INTO AN UNBREAKABLE GLASS WINDOW

In 1993, a Toronto lawyer named Garry Hoy, for unknown reasons, enjoyed showing onlookers how strong his office windows were by flinging his body into them. Hoy would always bounce off the window, *until one day he didn't.*

After throwing himself at the window once (a move that probably wasn't all that impressive to the visiting law students he was subjecting to his demonstrations), Hoy tested fate once more by hurling his body at the window again. This time, the window popped out of its frame, and Hoy fell 24 stories to his death.

Later, structural engineer Bob Greer explained to the *Toronto Star* that Hoy's faith in office windows was unfounded, stating, "I don't know of any building code in the world that would allow a 160-pound man to run up against a glass and withstand it."

PREMATURE BURIAL

Before modern science invented instruments to help doctors be 100 percent sure someone was dead, there was a higher-than-zero chance that people who were unconscious or comatose could be buried alive.

For obvious reasons, we have many more stories of people who luckily survived such mistakes than those who did not. For example, in the early 1600s, a woman named Marjorie Elphinstone was buried in Ardtannies, Scotland. Lucky for her, she was unintentionally revived by grave robbers who were after her jewelry. After her groans scared them away, Marjorie walked home and *outlived her spouse by six years*.

DEAD RINGER

In the late-18th and early-19th century, one could procure a "safety coffin," which included a bell system you could ring if accidentally buried alive. There are no records of a safety coffin saving someone, but there were many false alarms set off by swelling corpses.

Similarly, in the late-1500s, a man named Matthew Wall was being carried to his grave when one of the pallbearers tripped, **causing the casket to drop and jostling Wall into consciousness**. He lived for several more years and celebrated his "resurrection" annually until his actual death in 1595.

Risk of premature burial was at its height in the 17th century, when plague, cholera and smallpox were claiming lives left and right—apparently, *Monty Python and the Holy Grail*'s "I'm not dead yet" scene wasn't far off base. According to contemporary medical sources compiled by William Tebb, a British businessman who was ironically against vaccination and concerned about premature burial, there had been 219 near-cases of premature burial, 149 instances of definite premature burial, 10 people who were dissected before having died and two who had begun to be embalmed when they politely interrupted the proceedings.

KILLER CRITTERS

Anaconda
CBS News
Cobras.org
National Geographic

Asian Giant Hornet
AllThatsInteresting.com
National Geographic

Bear
ABC News
DailyItem.com
National Park Service

Bees
CNN
The Mayo Clinic

Blue Ringed Octopus
Fox News
Ocean Conservancy

Box Jellyfish
CNN
National Geographic
Science Magazine
Scientific American

Brazilian Wandering Spider
LiveScience.com
The Guardian

Brown Recluse Spider
Illinois Department of Public Health
LiveScience.com
VeryWellHealth.com

Bullet Ant
AllThatsInteresting.com
ThoughtCo.com

Canada Goose
GeeseRelief.com
USA Today

Cassowary
CNN
San Diego Zoo
Scientific American
The Guardian

Cats
Healthline.com
The Centers for Disease Control and Prevention
USA Today

Common Death Adder
ReptilePark.com.au

Cone Snail
AllThatsInteresting.com

Cow (Farting)
National Geographic

Cow (Falling)
The Telegraph

Crocodile
National Geographic
The Sun

Deathstalker Scorpion
Business Insider
LiveScience.com
New York-Presbyterian Hospital

Deer
USA Today
Vox

Dog
GreenvilleOnline.com
ScienceDirect.com

Dolphin
BBC
The Telegraph
Vox

Elephant
National Geographic

Giant Anteater
LiveScience.com
San Diego Zoo

Goat (Falling)
HurriyetDailyNews.com

Golden Poison Frog
BBC
National Geographic

Great White Shark
National Geographic
The Florida Museum of Natural History
The Guardian

Hippopotamus
BBC
National Geographic
The Washington Post

Horse
ABC News

Hyena
BBC
The Daily Mail

Inland Taipan Snake
LiveScience.com

Kissing Bug
Texas A&M University
The Centers for Disease
  Control and Prevention
WebMD.com

Komodo Dragon
Smithsonian Magazine
Smithsonian's National
  Zoo & Conservation
Biology Institute

Leopard
BBC
The Indian Express

Leopard Seal
National Geographic

Lion
Metro
National Geographic

Lionfish
National Geographic
The National Oceanic
  and Atmospheric
  Administration

Mosquito
MilfordBeacon.com
National Geographic
World Health Organization

Needlefish
MentalFloss.com
ThanhNienNews.com

Nile Monitor Lizard
The Atlantic
The Sun

Piranha
Encyclopedia Britannica
The Independent

Pufferfish
National Geographic
The Washington Post

Python
LiveScience.com
National Geographic
The New York Times

Rhinoceros
National Geographic
The Telegraph

Saw-Scaled Viper
Encyclopedia Britannica
National Geographic

Six-Eyed Sand Spider
AnimalCorner.co.uk

Slow Loris
National Geographic

Spitting Cobra
Daily Mirror
MentalFloss.com

Squirrel
Listverse.com

Stonefish
CNN
Forbes
Oceana
Queensland Museum

Stingray
HowStuffWorks.com
National Geographic

Striped Surgeonfish
Animal-World.com
Encyclopedia Britannica

Swan
BBC

Sweat Bees
BBC
The Atlantic

Sydney Funnel-Web Spider
Australian Geographic

Tiger
Smithsonian Magazine
Tigers of the World:
  The Science, Politics
  and Conservation of
  Panthera tigris, pages
  132–135

Tsetse Fly
BBC

📖 Sources

Tuna
Environmental Protection Agency
National Geographic

Wolf
The Star Tribune

PERILOUS PARASITES

Acanthamoeba
The Centers for Disease Control and Prevention

Ascaris Roundworm
MedicineNet.com
The Centers for Disease Control and Prevention

Bed Bugs
The Centers for Disease Control and Prevention
The Daily Mail

Botfly
LiveScience.com

Brain-Eating Amoeba
Popular Science

Enterobiasis Pinworm
The Centers for Disease Control and Prevention

Giant Kidney Worm
Stanford University
The Centers for Disease Control and Prevention

Gnathostoma
The Centers for Disease Control and Prevention

Guinea Worm
The Centers for Disease Control and Prevention
World Health Organization

Hookworm
PBS
The Centers for Disease Control and Prevention

Leishmania
The Centers for Disease Control and Prevention

Lice
Planned Parenthood
The Centers for Disease Control and Prevention

Liver Fluke
MedicalNewsToday.com
The Centers for Disease Control and Prevention

Lymphatic Filariasis
The Centers for Disease Control and Prevention
World Health Organization

Mango Fly
TripSavvy.com

Rat Lungworm
Popular Mechanics
The Centers for Disease Control and Prevention

Rhinosporidium Seeberi
Stanford University
The Centers for Disease Control and Prevention

Scabies
The Centers for Disease Control and Prevention

Schistosome
The Centers for Disease Control and Prevention

Screwworm
PBS

Spirometra Erinaceieuropaei
NewScientist.com
ScienceDirect.com

Tapeworm
AtlasObscura.com
The Mayo Clinic
Today.com

Ticks
The Centers for Disease Control and Prevention

Toxocara
The Centers for Disease Control and Prevention

Toxoplasmosis
The Centers for Disease Control and Prevention

Trichomonas Vaginalis
The Centers for Disease Control and Prevention

Whipworm
The Centers for Disease Control and Prevention

NATURAL DISASTERS

Avalanche
HowStuffWorks.com
Westword.com

Blizzard
LiveScience.com
Popular Science

Bog
smw.btck.co.uk
TripSavvy.com

Cliff
The Arizona Daily Sun

Deep Water
MedicalDaily.com
Slate.com
The National Oceanic and Atmospheric Administration

Door to Hell
National Geographic
Smithsonian Magazine

Drought
World Health Organization
World Meteorological Organization

Earthquake
National Geographic

Flood
Encyclopedia Britannica
National Geographic

Heat Wave
The Mayo Clinic
The Weather Channel

Hurricane
The National Oceanic and Atmospheric Administration
USA Today

Icicle
BBC
CityLab.com
The Chicago Tribune

Landslide
CNN
The Centers for Disease Control and Prevention
U.S. Geological Survey

Limnic Eruption
Curiosity.com
National Geographic
WorldAtlas.com

Lightning
Business Insider

Meteorite
American Meteor Society
National Geographic
Space.com
TheWeatherNetwork.com

Radon
Radon.com
The Centers for Disease Control and Prevention

Rip Current
Australian Geographic
OutsideOnline.com
The National Oceanic and Atmospheric Administration

River
ABC.net.au
The Buffalo News
The Miami Herald

Sun
BBC
Gizmodo.com
The New York Post
The Telegraph

Tornadoes
National Geographic

Tsunami
National Geographic

Quicksand
CBS News
National Geographic

Volcano
National Geographic

Wildfire
National Geographic
PBS

POISONOUS PLANTS

Ackee
IPSNews.net
Medscape.com
Time

Agave
HomeGuides.SFGate.com
Shanghaiist.com

Azalea
CNN
National Capital Poison Center
TheSpruce.com

Betel Nuts
BBC
Healthline.com

Bitter Almond
ATMPH.org
FoodSafetyNews.com
Livestrong.com
The Centers for Disease Control and Prevention

Caladium
North Carolina State University
U.S. National Library of Medicine

Cashew
Parade
The Telegraph
University of California, Davis

Cassava
The Guardian

Castor Beans
DelawareOnline.com
The Centers for Disease Control and Prevention
WebMD.com

Cherry Pits
Bon Appetit

Chili Pepper
Men's Health

Chinaberry Tree
fs.fed.us
Gardenerdy.com
TAndFOnline.com

Daffodil
National Capital Poison Center
Pharmacodynamic Basis of Herbal Medicine, By Manuchair Ebadi pg 297

Deadly Nightshade
CNN
Forbes
Slate
ThePoisonGarden.co.uk

Doll's Eye
IllinoisWildFlowers.info
MNN.com
North Carolina State University

Elderberry
Healthline.com

European Yew
ThePoisonGarden.co.uk
Wood-Database.com

Foxglove
AllinaHealth.org
National Capital Poison Center
Smithsonian Magazine
U.S. National Library of Medicine

Giant Hogweed
Good Housekeeping

Giant Pine Cone
ABC.net.au
The Los Angeles Times

Gympie-Gympie
Australian Geographic

Holly Berry
National Capital Poison Center
National Institutes of Health

Honey
Miel-Fou.com
ModernFarmer.com
National Capital Poison Center

Jimsonweed
Cornell University

Kidney Beans
Livestrong.com

Laetrile
WebMD.com

Manchineel Tree
AtlasObscura.com

Mistletoe
*National Capital Poison
Center
National Institutes of
Health
Smithsonian Magazine*

Mold
*FirstForWomen.com
MoldmanUSA.com*

Monkshood
*American Association for
Clinical Chemistry
National Capital Poison
Center
Phys.org*

Mushrooms
*National Capital Poison
Center*

Nettle
*Encyclopedia Britannica
Teara.govt.nz*

Nutmeg
*Delish
Healthline.com
NutritionFacts.org*

Oleander
University of Florida

Poinsettia
*American Society for the
Prevention of Cruelty to
Animals
National Capital Poison
Center
University of Illinois at
Urbana-Champaign*

Poison Hemlock
*National Capital Poison
Center
National Institutes of
Health*

Poison Ivy
*KidsHealth.org
ScienceDaily.com
TheGrowNetwork.com
The Mayo Clinic*

Potato
*Smithsonian Magazine
The New York Times*

Rhubarb Leaf
*DrAxe.com
National Geographic*

Rosary Pea
*National Institutes of
Health
The Centers for Disease
Control and Prevention*

Suicide Tree
*Curiosity.com
MentalFloss.com*

White Snakeroot
*National Park Service
Ohio State University*

DEADLY DISEASES & BACTERIA

Anthrax
*The Centers for Disease
Control and Prevention
The Mayo Clinic*

Balantidiasis
*The Centers for Disease
Control and Prevention*

Blastocystosis
*The Centers for Disease
Control and Prevention
The Mayo Clinic*

Brainerd Diarrhea
*The Centers for Disease
Control and Prevention*

Cancer
American Cancer Society
The Centers for Disease Control and Prevention

Cholera
The Mayo Clinic

CJD
The Centers for Disease Control and Prevention

COPD
The Centers for Disease Control and Prevention

Coronary Artery Disease
The Centers for Disease Control and Prevention

Dancing plague
PublicDomainReview.org

Dengue
The Centers for Disease Control and Prevention

Diabetes
The Centers for Disease Control and Prevention

E. coli
The Centers for Disease Control and Prevention

Ebola
National Geographic
The Centers for Disease Control and Prevention
World Health Organization

Fatal Familial Insomnia
Medium.com
National Organization for Rare Disorders

Gangrene
The Mayo Clinic

Gonorrhea
STDCheck.com
The Centers for Disease Control and Prevention

Group A Strep
The Centers for Disease Control and Prevention

Hantavirus
The Centers for Disease Control and Prevention

Hepatitis
The Centers for Disease Control and Prevention
World Health Organization

HIV
The Centers for Disease Control and Prevention
U.S. Department of Health and Human Services

Influenza
CBS News
The History Channel

Leprosy
National Park Service
The Centers for Disease Control and Prevention

Listeria
The Centers for Disease Control and Prevention

Mad Cow Disease
HowStuffWorks.com
The Centers for Disease Control and Prevention
WebMD.com

Meningitis
DailyVoice.com
The Mayo Clinic
WebMD.com

Middle East Respiratory Syndrome
The Centers for Disease Control and Prevention

Necrotizing Fasciitis
The Centers for Disease Control and Prevention

Noma
Pan American Health Organization
U.S. National Library of Medicine

Plague
National Geographic
The Centers for Disease Control and Prevention
The Mayo Clinic
World Health Organization

Pneumonia
The Centers for Disease Control and Prevention
The Mayo Clinic

Rabies
The Centers for Disease
Control and Prevention
World Health Organization

Salmonella
The Centers for Disease
Control and Prevention

Scurvy
BetterHealth.vic.gov.au
LiveScience.com

Severe Acute
Respiratory Syndrome
The Centers for Disease
Control and Prevention
The Mayo Clinic

Smallpox
The Centers for Disease
Control and Prevention

Syphilis
ScienceDaily.com
Smithsonian Magazine
The Centers for Disease
Control and Prevention

Trachoma
The Centers for Disease
Control and Prevention

Tuberculosis
JMVH.org
The Centers for Disease
Control and Prevention
University of Virginia
World Health Organization

West Nile Virus
The Centers for Disease
Control and Prevention

Yellow Fever
The Centers for Disease
Control and Prevention
World Health Organization

PERSONAL FAILINGS

Allergies
The Mayo Clinic

Aneurysm
American Heart
Association
Brain Aneurysm
Foundation

Apotemnophilia
Scientific American
University of California
San Diego

Aquagenic Urticaria
National Institutes of
Health
People

Blood Clot
U.S. National Library of
Medicine

Boredom
MentalFloss.com
The Telegraph

Brittle Bone Disease
National Institute
of Arthritis and
Musculoskeletal and Skin
Diseases

Bursting Bladder
LiveScience.com
Popular Science

Celiac
Celiac Disease Foundation

Cold Urticaria
The Mayo Clinic

Dying From Laughter
BBC
BMJ.com
Snopes.com

Ehlers-Danlos
Syndrome
National Institutes of
Health
The Sun

Fear
Fox News
Scientific American

Hemophilia
The Mayo Clinic

Holding in a Sneeze
National Institute on Drug
Abuse
The Telegraph

Sources

Lupus
The Mayo Clinic

Pica
National Eating Disorders Association

Rapunzel Syndrome
LiveScience.com

Stone Man Syndrome
RareDiseaseReview.org

Tree Man Syndrome
AllThatsInteresting.com
MedicalXpress.com

Trimethylaminuria
National Institutes of Health
National Organization for Rare Disorders
The Daily Mail

Vampire Syndrome
The Mayo Clinic

Walking Corpse Syndrome
Healthline.com
Psychology Today
Smithsonian Magazine

HUMAN-MADE MISERY

Alcohol
Harvard Health Publishing, Harvard Medical School
U.S. News

Antibiotic Resistance
World Health Organization

Anti-Vaxxers
Huffington Post
SBS.com.au

Asbestos
Asbestos.com, The Mesothelioma Center
Oregon State University
TheDenverChannel.com

BPAs
Healthline.com
The Mayo Clinic

Chubby Bunny
Snopes.com

Cigarettes (Cancer)
BuzzFeed
St. Petersburg Times, October 31, 1975
The Centers for Disease Control and Prevention

Climate Change
Center for American Progress Action Fund
Global Climate Change, National Aeronautics and Space Administration
The Climate Reality Project
The Weather Channel

Coal Emissions
Union of Concerned Scientists

Cocaine
National Institute on Drug Abuse
The Guardian
WebMD.com

Diesel Engine Exhaust
The Occupational Safety and Health Administration

Diet Pills
HeraldScotland.com
The Pharmaceutical Journal

Eating Yourself to Death
AllThatsInteresting.com
NBC News
Ranker.com

Fruit Juice Injection
The New York Post
WHFoods.com

Heating a Lava Lamp
Snopes.com

Lead
CNN
World Health Organization

Man-Made Floods
Smithsonian Magazine
The History Channel

Margarine
Harvard Health
Publishing, Harvard
Medical School
Healthline.com

Mercury Poisoning
The History Channel
Vox

Microwave Popcorn
American Lung
Association
CBS News
Healthline.com
The New York Times

Muslin Disease
The Daily Beast

Opioids
KnowTheDangers.com
National Institute on Drug
Abuse
World Health Organization

Pesticides
Environmental Protection
Agency
Pesticide Action Network
U.K.
PesticideFacts.org

Planking
CBS News
Fox News

Plastic Caps
ScienceAlert.com
The New York Times
The Telegraph

Pokémon Go
NBC News
Ranker.com
Sky News

Premature Burial
HistoryCollection.co
Snopes.com

rBGH
Grist.org
ThinkBeforeYouPink.org

Red and Processed Meats
American Cancer Society
Cancer Research U.K.

Running Into an Unbreakable Glass Window
Snopes.com

Selfie
OutsideOnline.com
Rolling Stone

Shooting a Protected Cactus
Snopes.com
University of Arkansas

Storm Drains
HowStuffWorks.com
People

Tanning Beds
American Academy of
Dermatology
Skin Cancer Foundation

Tide Pods
Harvard Health
Publishing, Harvard
Medical School

Tripping on Your Own Beard
AtlasObscura.com

Vending Machine
Journal of Orthopaedic
Trauma
The Guardian

Video Game Addiction
CNN
TaipeiTimes.com
The Mayo Clinic

Water Intoxication
Scientific American

Yellowstone Hot Springs
Huffington Post
National Park Service

Media Lab Books
For inquiries, call 646-838-6637

Copyright 2020 Topix Media Lab

Published by Topix Media Lab
14 Wall Street, Suite 4B
New York, NY 10005

Manufactured in Singapore

ISBN-13: 978-1-948174-38-1
ISBN-10: 1-948174-38-3